CUPCAKES
& MINI CAKES

CUPCAKES
& MINI CAKES

LONDON, NEW YORK, MELBOURNE, MUNICH, AND DELHI

Project Editor Elizabeth Yeates
Designer Alison Shackleton
Jacket Designer Mark Penfound
Managing Editor Dawn Henderson
Managing Art Editor Christine Keilty
Special Sales Creative Project Manager
Alison Donovan
Pre-Production Producer Ray Williams
Senior Producer Jen Scothern
Publisher Peggy Vance

First published in Great Britain in 2015
by Dorling Kindersley Limited
80 Strand, London WC2R 0RL

Material in this publication was previously published in:
Easy World Baking Small Cakes and Desserts (2013),
Easy World Baking Patisserie (2013), Easy World Baking
Traybakes (2013), Everyday Easy Cakes (2013),
Cake Decorating (2013)

A Penguin Random House Company

A CIP catalogue record for this book is available
from the British Library.

ISBN 978-0-2410-0972-7

Printed and bound in China
by Hung Hing Off-set Printing Co., Ltd

Discover more at **www.dk.com**

Contents

Recipe chooser   6

Techniques   18

Cupcakes and Muffins   58

Mini cakes
and Cake pops   102

Mini bakes and Slices   142

Patisserie and Tarts   188

Index   252

Celebration

Chocolate and vanilla whoopie pies page 124

Blueberry and pistachio angel cupcakes page 72

Raspberry macarons page 200

Mini banana and chocolate topped cheesecakes page 110

Cupcake bouquet page 100

Coffee kisses page 172

Cherry flapjacks page 156

Orange and lemon cupcakes page 76

Butterflies and blossoms
page 96

Wedding mini cakes
page 128

Strawberry shortcakes
page 122

White chocolate and macadamia nut blondies
page 146

White chocolate and coconut snowballs page 134

Vanilla cupcakes
page 66

Celebration   7

Weekend brunch

Lemon and blueberry muffins
page 94

Cinnamon palmiers
page 192

Hot cross buns
page 246

Danish pastries
page 196

Pains au chocolat
page 244

Pistachio and orange biscotti
page 186

Apple muffins
page 62

Almond crescents
page 228

Croissants aux amandes
page 248

Cinnamon rolls
page 230

Apricot pastries
page 216

Great for kids

Scary cake pops
page 139

Chocolate and hazelnut brownies page 166

Fondant fancies
page 118

Chocolate and toffee shortbread page 174

Chocolate cupcakes
page 60

Toffee brownies
page 148

Raspberry flapjacks
page 178

Pirate cake pops
page 140

Sticky date flapjacks
page 152

Christmas cake pops
page 138

Sticky walnut buns
page116

Cherry and coconut cupcakes
page 80

Chocolate lovers

Chocolate truffles
page 202

Chocolate orange profiteroles
page 238

Chocolate muffins
page 78

Chocolate fondants
page 106

Chocolate palmiers
page 206

Chocolate fudge cake balls

page 132

Chocolate biscuit cake

page 184

Triple chocolate crunch bars

page 170

Chocolate cupcakes

page 60

Chocolate lovers **13**

Afternoon tea

Coffee walnut cupcakes
page 84

Chocolate palmiers
page 206

White chocolate cakes
page 104

**Raspberry, lemon, and almond
bake** page 162

**Strawberries amd cream
whoopie pies** page 108

Florentine slices
page 158

Strawberry and cream cupcakes page 92

Apricot crumble shortbread page 168

Lime drizzle cupcakes page 70

Berry friands page 88

Raspberry tartlets with crème pâtissère page 194

Tangerine macarons page 224

After dinner

Chocolate brittle
page 182

Toffee apple traybake
page 164

White chocolate cakes
page 104

Sour cherry and chocolate brownies
page 176

Profiteroles
page 220

Apple and almond galettes
page 242

Mocha slices
page 154

Banana and Nutella crumble tartlets
page 204

Sticky toffee puddings
page 120

Coconut cream tartlets
page 212

Techniques

Baking ingredients

Understanding your ingredients and how to use them will improve your baking. Always measure carefully and never mix metric and imperial measurements.

Ingredient	Choose	Use
Butter	Both salted or unsalted butter can be used for baking. Unsalted butter is mostly preferred in this book, but it's all down to taste preference, and whether you are reducing the salt in your diet. The amount of salt in salted butter varies, so check the label. Salted butter will keep for longer if you keep it in a butter dish out of the refrigerator.	Salted or unsalted, for cakes and bakes. Use softened butter (at room temperature). This means plenty of air will be held by the fat as you mix, making your cake or bake lighter.
Sugar	Caster sugar is finer than granulated. Use unrefined sugar (golden caster sugar) if you can. It is more natural than white refined sugar, which is processed and stripped of its molasses. Unrefined sugar adds a slight caramel flavour to your baking. "Brown" sugar is also white refined sugar, but it has the molasses added back to it.	Caster sugar, unrefined if possible, for cakes and bakes. White and brown sugars are equally sweet but the molasses in brown sugar create a moister texture.
Baking powder	This is a raising agent used in baking. It is a mixture of bicarbonate of soda and cream of tartar, a natural raising agent, and is different to baking soda or bicarbonate of soda, as it doesn't contain cream of tartar. The two cannot be interchanged. Check the sell-by date of baking powder, as its effect wears off when it's old.	Cakes and biscuits. If a recipe calls for self-raising flour and you haven't got any, add baking powder to plain flour (4 tsp per 225g (8oz)).

Ingredient	Choose	Use

Flour

Plain flour and self-raising flour are quite low in gluten, unlike strong bread flour. There are many flours that are suitable for a wheat-free or gluten-free diet, such as rice flour, chestnut flour, and potato flour. If using, consult specialist recipes as they are not interchangeable with plain flour.

Plain flour or self-raising flour, sifted, for cakes and bakes. Don't over-beat once flour has been added, as the gluten will strengthen and you'll get a tough texture. This is why flour is folded in.

Eggs

Choose organic and/or free-range hens' eggs, as they will improve the flavour and quality of your finished cake.

Use at room temperature. If they are used cold from the refrigerator, they cool the butter down and the mixture can curdle.

A guide to symbols

The recipes in this book are accompanied by symbols that alert you to important information.

 Tells you how many people the recipe serves, or how much is produced.

 Indicates how much time you will need to prepare and cook a dish. Next to this symbol you will also find out if additional time is required for such things as chilling, soaking, or proving. Read the recipe to find out exactly how much extra time to allow.

 This denotes that special equipment is required, such as a springform tin or special mould. Where possible, alternatives are given.

 This symbol accompanies freezing information.

Equipment

Baking

Square/round baking tins
Depending upon your project, you'll need good-quality, non-stick pans to produce great cakes that just tip out of the tin.

Cake-pop sticks
These come in a number of colours and sizes. As long as they are 'food safe' anything goes.

Measuring spoons
Essential for the little additions that make a perfect cake.

Cake-pop tin
These are a wonderful addition to the market. Grease them carefully and allow the pops to cool in place before tipping out.

Cooling rack for cakes
Essential for cooling cakes and cupcakes of every description. Let your cakes cool in the pan for 10 minutes, and then tip out.

Cupcake cases
Cases don't just support your cupcakes while baking, but also help to provide a theme!

Cupcake tins
Tiny and full-sized cupcakes will always require a good tin! Always choose liners that fit!

Sugar thermometer
If you are making a fancy meringue icing or need to temper your chocolate, you'll need a thermometer to ensure ingredients reach the right temperature.

Measuring jug
Most cakes have liquid ingredients that will need to be measured.

Timer
Don't underestimate the importance of timing! Set your timer for every project.

Wooden spoon
A kitchen standby, for mixing virtually anything.

Sharp knife
Required for decorations, cutting cakes, and almost every element of cake making and decorating.

Scales
All ingredients have to be carefully measured, and scales are a must.

Equipment

Decorating

Cutters
Use cutters to make your decorations more precise. Dust them with corn flour first to allow easy releasing.

Palette knife
Essential both for crumb-coating and simple cupcake icing.

Edible felt-tip pens
Use in numerous colours and with different-sized tips for fine or bold painting or lettering.

Paintbrushes
Choose synthetic paintbrushes that will not lose their bristles, in a variety of sizes, with small brushes for fine details and larger ones for painting expanses of colour and dusting.

Non-stick fondant mat
This helps to roll out fondant easily and prevents sticking.

Fondant smoother
Use to smooth decorations, boards, or cake toppings. Use two to achieve crisp corners and edges.

Fondant roller
A non-stick roller will make handling fondant much easier.

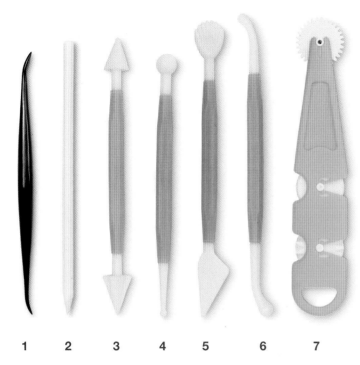

1 Veining (or Dresden) tools
Add detail to fondant or paste decorations.

2 Frilling tools
Create frills and ruffles to rolled fondant.

3 Cone tools
Create detail and texture. They double up as star embossers.

4 Ball tools
Can thin and soften edges to create petal shapes and contours.

5 Shell and blade tools
Emboss shell patterns and texture, and can cut or shape.

6 Bone tools
Smooth curves when modelling, and cup flower petals.

7 Stitching (quilting)
Tools emboss decorations and cakes with stitching effects.

Piping bag and tips, plus coupler
Any type of bag will work and if you are stuck you can also use a sandwich bag with the corner cut out and a tip inserted. Tip sizes are important; smaller numbers mean tinier tips.

Test eggs for freshness

As well as the best-before date on the egg box, you can use this simple test to check how fresh your eggs are: immerse the egg in water and see if it rises. A stale egg contains much more air and less liquid than a fresh one, so it will float. Do not use a stale egg.

Fresh

Borderline

Stale

Separate eggs

Many recipes call for either yolks or whites. Smell the eggs first to be sure they are fresh, or use the floating test above.

1 Break the shell of a cold egg by tapping it against the rim of a bowl. Insert your fingers into the break and gently pry the two halves apart.

2 Gently shift the yolk back and forth between the shell halves, allowing the white to separate and fall into the bowl. Take care to keep the yolk intact.

Whisk egg whites

For the best results, use a clean, dry glass or metal bowl and a balloon whisk.
The whites must be completely free of yolk, or any other contact with grease.

1 Place the egg whites in the bowl (here a copper bowl is used) and begin whisking slowly, using a small range of motion.

2 Continue whisking steadily, using larger strokes, until the whites have lost their translucency and start to foam

3 Incorporating as much air as possible, increase your speed and range of motion until the whites peak to the desired degree and are stiff but not dry.

4 Test by lifting the whisk; the peaks should be firm but glossy and the tips should hang.

Prepare and line a cake tin

Greasing then flouring or lining your tin ensures that baked layers turn out cleanly and easily.

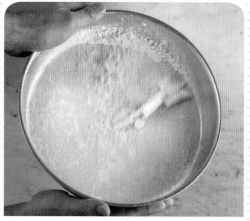

1 Melt unsalted butter (unless your recipe states otherwise) and use a pastry brush to apply a thin, even layer over the bottom and sides of the tin, making sure to brush butter into the corners.

2 Then, sprinkle a small amount of flour into the tin. Shake the pan so the flour coats the bottom and rotate the tin to coat the sides. Turn the tin upside down and tap to remove the excess flour.

3 Or, to line with baking parchment instead of flour, stand the tin on the paper and draw around the base with a pencil. Cut out the shape just inside the pencil line.

4 Place the piece of baking parchment directly on to the greased bottom of the cake tin. It should fit neatly inside and into the corners. This layer can be peeled off once your cake is cooked and cooled.

Prepare chocolate

Chill the chocolate before cutting and grating, as the warmth of your hands will quickly melt it.

For chopping, break the chocolate into small pieces, then chill the pieces in the freezer for a few minutes. Place on a cutting board and use a sharp knife to chop using a rocking motion.

For grating, rub chilled chocolate against the face of the grater, using the widest holes. If the chocolate begins to melt, chill it again in the freezer and continue grating once it has hardened.

To melt chocolate, gently simmer some water in a pan. Place chopped chocolate in a heatproof bowl and set it over the water. Let the chocolate melt, then it stir with a wooden spoon until smooth.

For curls, spread soft or melted chocolate on to a cool marble surface. Use the blade of a large knife to scrape the chocolate into curls.

Chocolate

A versatile ingredient that you can use for many decorating techniques, chocolate can be temperamental, so follow instructions carefully.

Making ganache

Ganache is simply chocolate melted into cream, which is then whisked to silky perfection. It can be poured over a cake while warm, or left to cool and spread with a palette knife.

• makes 500g
(1lb 2oz)

• prep 5 mins
• cook 5 mins

Ingredients

200ml (7fl oz)
double cream
200g (7oz) good-
quality dark, milk,
or white chocolate

1 Break the chocolate into pieces and place it with the cream in a medium heavy-bottomed pan. Stir over a low heat until the chocolate has melted.

2 Remove from the heat, transfer to a heatproof bowl, and whisk until glossy and thick. Pour over the cake or leave to cool for 1–2 hours before spreading.

Whip cream

Depending on your recipe, you can whip to soft or stiff peaks. Remember to chill the whisk, bowl, and cream beforehand.

1 Remove the cream from the refrigerator and let it reach the temperature of 5°C (40°F). Start whipping slowly with about 2 strokes per second (or the lowest speed on an electric whisk) until the cream begins to thicken. Increase the whipping to a moderate speed for soft peaks.

2 For stiff peaks, continue beating the cream for some time. Test by lifting the beaters to see if the cream retains its shape.

Pipe with a bag and nozzle

This technique can be used not only for piping cream, but also for meringue, pastry, and sorbet. Use a variety of nozzles to create interesting designs.

1 Place the nozzle in the bag, then give it a twist to seal and prevent leakage.

2 Holding the bag just above the nozzle with one hand, fold the top of the bag over with your other hand, creating a "collar", and begin spooning in the cream.

3 Continue filling, until the bag is three-quarters full. Twist the top of the bag to clear any air pockets. The cream should be just visible in the tip of the nozzle.

4 Holding the twisted end of the bag taut in one hand, use your other hand to gently press the filling to start a steady flow, and direct the nozzle as desired.

Making cupcakes

Be sure to fill the tins or cases properly and cook for the correct length of time. Always preheat the oven for at least 20 minutes. Prepare the tins before you begin to make the batter, so that it doesn't begin to rise before you put it into the cases.

Using cases

Cupcake cases add a decorative element, make the cupcakes look neater, and help them remain fresh and moist for longer. If you choose to use a cupcake tin on its own, grease and dust it, brush with cake release products, or spray with a non-stick baking spray. Silicone cases do not require a cupcake tin. Fill and set them upright on a baking tray. Grease and dust them with plain flour to ensure that the cupcakes do not stick.

Filling

Fill the cupcake cases or tins about two-thirds full. Do not overfill as they can spill over the sides or develop a "nose". Standard-sized cupcakes require about 75ml (2½fl oz) of batter. For mini cupcakes, a heaped tablespoon of batter is enough. For special effects, layer different colours of batter into the cases with a piping bag. Create a surprise centre by popping sweets or even a biscuit or a miniature brownie into the centre before cooking.

Baking

A standard-sized cupcake will take 18–20 minutes to bake, while mini cupcakes will take 8–10 minutes. They are ready if a skewer inserted in the middle of the cake comes out clean. When baking several tins at the same time, increase the baking time by a few minutes, and rotate the trays halfway through. Allow to cool in the tin for at least 10 minutes and then cool on a wire rack. If you do not use cases, turn the cupcakes out onto your hand before placing them on the rack.

Baking miniature cakes

Make miniature ("mini") cakes in the same way as cupcakes, but bake them in specially designed round or square cake tins. Grease and dust the tins carefully. You could use deep cutters or a knife to cut mini cakes from a large cake, but this is not as accurate and you may waste cake.

1 Preheat the oven to 180°C (350°F/Gas 4). Whisk the butter and sugar until fluffy. Mix in the eggs one at a time. Whisk for 2 minutes more, until bubbles appear on the surface. Sift in the flour, add the zest, and fold in until just smooth.

2 Fill all of the tins with the same amount of batter – roughly half to two-thirds full. Depending on their size, bake for 15-25 minutes.

3 When they look like they may be done, test every two minutes until a skewer comes out clean. Allow the cakes to cool in the tins and then turn out onto a wire rack.

Ingredients

175g (6oz) unsalted butter, softened
175g (6oz) caster sugar
3 eggs
225g (8oz) self-raising flour
grated zest of 1 lemon

- makes 16

- prep 20 mins
- cook 15 mins

- 16 x 5cm (2in) mini round cake tins

Divide the mix equally between the tins. Trim the cakes when they have cooled, if necessary.

Tip
Bake cupcakes as soon as the batter is ready. This will ensure that the air in the mixture does not escape, resulting in flatter cupcakes. Cupcakes and mini cakes can be decorated, once cool, with a variety of toppings.

Piping cupcakes

You could ice a cupcake with buttercream icing using a palette knife, rotating it on a flat surface as you spread. For a quick, professional-looking finish, however, pipe the buttercream into a swirl, as shown here. You could use different tips for stars, shells, or a variety of effects and textures.

• piping bag with large open-star tip

Ingredients

buttercream icing (see p38)
cooled cupcakes
sprinkles or edible glitter, optional

1 Attach the tip to the piping bag and fill it half full with medium-consistency icing. More makes the bag difficult to handle.

2 Hold the tip 1cm (½in) above the cupcake, at a 90° angle, and pipe from the outside edge inwards, in a spiral.

3 Apply pressure so that an even quantity is released. Slowly increase the pressure at the centre, so that the icing forms a peak.

4 Release the pressure to end the spiral at the centre of the cupcake. Decorate with sprinkles or edible glitter, if desired.

...use different tips for a variety of effects and textures

Filling cupcakes

Cupcakes can be filled with jam, buttercream icing, ganache, cream, or even loosened peanut butter, fruit mousses, and curds. Pop in a marshmallow or another treat before filling, for an extra surprise. There are two successful methods for filling cakes with liquid ingredients.

Cone method

With a sharp paring knife, cut out a cone shape from the centre of each cupcake. Slice off the tip of the cone, fill the cone-shaped cavity in the cupcake to just below the top, and then replace the flat end of the cone on top. Proceed to ice as usual (see opposite).

Piping method

If you have thin, smooth icing or jam, you can use a plain round tip (pictured below) or a specialized injector tip on a piping bag. Attach the tip, load the piping bag with filling, and then insert it into the centre of the cupcake, from the top. Gently press on the bag until the filling begins to expand out of the insertion hole. Proceed to ice and decorate as usual (see opposite).

Using a piping bag helps to control the amount of filling you use.

Tip
Always make sure the cupcakes are completely cool before attempting to fill them or they will fall apart. Cooling will also ensure that the filling will not melt into the cupcake, making it soggy and messy to eat.

Making cake pops

Cake pops are relative newcomers to the baking arena and offer a perfect opportunity to accessorize cakes and create a decorative theme. There are two ways to make cake pops. This method uses up leftover cake – easily moulded into balls, hearts, or even critters.

• makes 20–25

• prep 4 hrs

• 25 cake-pop sticks
• florist oasis or Styrofoam

Ingredients

300g (10oz) chocolate cake crumbs
150g (5½oz) chocolate buttercream icing (see p38)
250g (9oz) dark chocolate cake covering
50g (1¾oz) white chocolate
300g (10oz) candy melts (optional, to replace dark and white chocolate)
sprinkles, nuts, or ground wafers, to decorate, optional

1 Place the cake crumbs in a large bowl, and stir in the buttercream icing, mixing until you have a smooth dough.

2 Using your hands, gently mould the mixture into uniform balls, each the approximate size of a walnut.

3 Place on a plate, with space between each, and refrigerate for 3 hours; alternatively, you can freeze for 30 minutes.

To cover
Line two trays with baking parchment and melt some dark chocolate covering. Dip one end of a cake-pop stick into the chocolate and insert into the centre of each pop. Stand them upright in florist oasis for 30 minutes. Melt the rest of the chocolate covering and white chocolate, or candy melts. Dip the pops into the chocolate and swirl to cover. Allow excess to drip off, and dip them in sprinkles, nuts, or ground wafers, if desired.

Using a cake-pop tin

Cake-pop tins create uniform balls that are ready to dip and decorate. Light sponges are not dense enough to support the weight of the pop on a stick, or the decorations. Madeira cake is a better option. Most cake-pop tins come with recipes.

1 Preheat the oven to 180°C (350°F/Gas 4). Whisk the butter and sugar until fluffy. Mix in the eggs, one at a time. Whisk for 2 minutes more, until bubbles appear on the surface. Sift in the flour, add the zest, and fold in until smooth.

2 Grease and dust the cake-pop tins. Spoon the batter into the bottom half of the tin (without holes) so that it mounds over the top. Place the top half of the tin on top and secure.

3 Bake for 15–18 minutes. Allow the cakes to cool in the tin for 10 minutes and then turn out onto a wire rack to cool completely.

4 Dip one end of a cake-pop stick into the melted chocolate and insert into the centre of each pop. Chill for 20–30 minutes, with the sticks upright.

Ingredients

175g (6oz) unsalted
  butter, softened
175g (6oz) caster sugar
3 eggs
225g (8oz) self-raising
  flour
grated zest of 1 lemon
plain flour, for dusting
melted chocolate

• makes 24

• prep 20 mins
• cook 15–18 mins

• 2 x 12-hole
cake-pop tins

Tip

To keep the chocolate or candy melts warm and in a liquid state while dipping, use a fondue pot or place the pan on a tea-light burner. Using a taller, narrow pan makes dipping easier and much less messy.

Bake the cake pops until a skewer comes out clean.

Buttercream icing

This type of icing is made with butter, icing sugar, and cream or milk, and is lightly flavoured with vanilla or another flavouring. Use it to ice and fill sponge cakes and cupcakes. Some buttercreams require cooking, but most can be whipped up quickly with an electric whisk.

Basic vanilla buttercream icing

You can make this with or without cream or milk. It is ideal for crumb coating, icing sponge cakes, and for piping onto cupcakes. You could also use it for brushwork embroidery (see p49).

- makes 750g (1lb 10oz)
- prep 15–20 mins

Ingredients

250g (9oz) unsalted butter, softened
2 tsp vanilla extract
600g (1lb 5oz) icing sugar
2 tbsp double cream or milk, plus extra for thinning
colouring paste, optional

1 Cream the butter and vanilla together with an electric whisk. Add the icing sugar, beating well.

2 Beat in the cream and continue mixing until the icing is light and fluffy.

3 Transfer to a bowl and add colouring paste, a little at a time, until you get the right colour.

4 The icing should be firm enough to hold a knife upright, but soft enough to be piped.

Tip
To make chocolate buttercream, add 8 tbsp of cocoa powder after step 2 and beat until fluffy. Use milk instead of cream in step 2. If you prefer a lighter flavour, halve the amount of cocoa powder, and add at step 1.

Royal icing

This type of icing is traditionally used to ice fruitcakes for weddings or Christmas, and to decorate gingerbread houses. To use for decorative piping, make the same way, but without the glycerine, and whisk to a smooth consistency.

Traditional royal icing

Royal icing dries hard, so keep it covered with cling film or a damp towel while you are working. The glycerine in this recipe stops the icing from becoming rock hard, and provides a little shine.

Ingredients

3 free-range
   pasteurized egg
   whites; albumen
   powder, mixed with
   water; or meringue
   powder
700g (1¾lb) icing
   sugar, sifted, plus
   extra if needed
1 tsp lemon juice
2 tsp glycerine
fruitcake, levelled and
   layered if desired,
   covered with
   marzipan

1 Whisk the egg whites in a large bowl until they are foamy. Add the icing sugar a spoonful at a time.

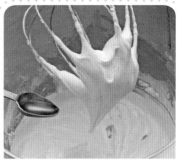

2 Stir in the lemon juice and glycerine, and beat until stiff, thick, and peaks begin to form.

3 To ice a cake, add more icing sugar to thicken, if necessary. Use a palette knife to spread on the top and sides of your cake, as you would with buttercream icing (see opposite). Use an icing scraper, as shown with a mini cake, to provide a smooth finish. Try a serrated scraper for a uniform texture.

• makes 750g
(1lb 10oz)

• prep 15 mins

• scraper or
serrated scraper,
optional

Piping buttercream borders

Buttercream is an excellent medium for piping decorative borders or effects. You can pipe figures, flowers, and other decorations, and even use it for brushwork embroidery (see p49). Get the consistency of the buttercream right (see p38), and use the correct tips.

• piping bag fitted with an open star tip (such as Wilton no. 21), filled with buttercream icing (see p38)

Ingredients

round smooth-iced cake on a fondant-covered cake drum

1 **For a shell border**, hold the bag at a 45° angle just above the cake surface. Squeeze, so that the icing fans out.

2 Relax the pressure, and pull the bag along the base of the cake. Pull the tip along to form a point. Repeat.

Tip

If the buttercream has air bubbles after beating, press them out against the sides of the bowl with a spatula to help you to get a smooth product. Avoid overfilling the bag, as it will warm in your hands and the icing will melt.

For drop flowers, hold the bag directly above the cake surface, just touching. Squeeze, letting the icing build up to make a flower. Stop squeezing and lift the tip away. You could turn the hand that is holding the bag as you squeeze out the icing for a swirl, and/or add a dragée to the centre.

Buttercream is excellent for piping borders or effects

Piping a buttercream rose

Pipe a simple rose using buttercream icing. It can be piped directly onto a small square of baking parchment, onto a cake in a single, flowing movement (see Variation), or piped onto a flower nail, as shown here, and then applied to the cake when the buttercream has firmed a little.

1 Hold the tip above the centre of the flower nail. Apply pressure and squeeze out a cone shape of icing.

2 Change to a petal tip. Hold the bag at a 45° angle and squeeze to form a ribbon of icing that overlaps at the top of the cone.

• piping bag, fitted with a coupler and a round tip (such as Wilton no. 12), filled with buttercream icing (see p38)
• petal tip (such as Wilton no. 104)
• flower nail

3 Place the wide end of the tip against the base of the bud. Squeeze and move the tip up and then down to the base. Repeat for 3 petals around the bud, overlapping each petal just behind the edge of the first. Repeat the same technique, creating a row of 5 petals and finally a row of 7, angling the tip to create an open rose.

Variation

To pipe a buttercream rose with a single movement, attach a large or medium open star tip to your piping bag. Pipe a dab of buttercream to create a centre, and then carefully work your way around the centre in an anticlockwise motion to create a swirl.

Piping dots, beads, and flowers

Decorate the top of a cupcake with a series of simple piped royal icing picot dots, beads, and flowers. Picot is a type of elegant "embroidery" that can be undertaken with a series of small, simply piped dots. For a different effect that is as easy to achieve, try a beaded border.

• piping bag fitted with a small, round tip (such as Wilton no. 1L), filled with piping-consistency royal icing (see p39)

Ingredients

fondant-covered or royal-iced cake

For picot dots, hold the bag so the tip is just above the cake. Pipe a dot, increasing pressure to increase its size. Stop squeezing to drop it.

For beads, hold the bag at a 45° angle. Apply pressure as you lift to allow the icing to spread out. Stop the pressure as you drop it.

For flowers, prepare the bag as before. Pipe a small dot and then push the point of the tip into the edge and drag it towards you in a petal shape. Continue, piping another dot beside the first one, working in a circle, until you form a flower.

Tip

When piping picot dots, do not gradually stop the pressure, or you will get a "nose" on the dot. Instead, stop squeezing and pull away immediately. Allow to dry just slightly, dip your finger in a little cornflour, and gently press it down.

Melting and tempering in a microwave

This takes less time than the traditional method but it may take some practice, as you will have far less control of the heat. As with the traditional method, it is best to use a specialized sugar thermometer to test the temperature regularly. Overheating will cause the chocolate to take a "white bloom" once hard. Chocolate should be lukewarm to pipe effectively. Temper the chocolate for the shiniest and hardest results.

1 Break the chocolate into squares, place it in a microwavable bowl, and heat on full power for 30 seconds. Stir, and heat again in 15-second bursts until the chocolate is smooth and melted.

Ingredients

500g (1lb 2oz) good-quality milk, dark, or white chocolate

- makes 500g (1lb 2oz)

- prep 5 mins, plus cooling
- cook 5 mins

- sugar thermometer

2 Test the temperature and continue to heat in short bursts until it reaches 45°C (113°F). Allow to cool until the temperature reaches 27°C (80°F), stirring frequently. The chocolate should remain at this temperature as you use it, for instance for wrapping a cake (see Variation). Warm it a little if it drops too low.

Variation

To wrap an iced cake, spread tempered chocolate over acetate that is a little larger in size than the circumference of your cake, and a little wider than its height. As the chocolate begins to harden, wrap it around the cake. When it is hard, remove the acetate.

Piping with buttercream icing

Much softer than royal icing, pipe buttercream with any tip and in any colour to create a wide variety of decorative effects on iced cakes or cake drums. It's perfect for cupcakes, too. Varying the size of the tip and the pressure you apply can change the design dramatically.

Shell border

Use a medium open star tip for a shell border. Allow the icing to fan out as you drag and drop.

Zigzag border

An open star tip can create an attractive pattern that works well on the surface of cakes.

Swirl border

Use an open star tip to create a series of interlinked, scroll-like swirls.

Dot border

Create a row of symmetrical dots or beads with a medium round tip.

Stars and star border

Create individual stars (below) or link them together as a border, using a medium open star tip.

Piped leaves

Use a small leaf tip to create leaves, ruffling the lengths and dragging the piped icing to a tip.

Basketweave

A medium basketweave tip is used here, with small sections of piping in a woven pattern over longer lines of buttercream.

Grass

Short strands of grass (and even fur or hair) can be created with a small multi-opening grass tip.

Longer grass

Pipe longer, wider strands of buttercream with a medium multi-opening grass tip to create grass and individual hair strands.

Rosette border

Use a medium open star tip to swirl tiny rosettes that can be linked or used individually.

Pulled bead border

Use a medium round tip to pipe beads and then slowly release the pressure as you drag each bead.

C-scroll border

Linking up a series of "C"s, using a small open star tip, creates an easy and pretty border; alternate "C"s with "S"s for a different look.

Rope border

Create a sturdy rope or a series of scrolls by linking a series of backwards "S"s with a medium open star tip.

Ruffle border

Pipe a simple ruffled border using a medium petal tip, dragging the icing back on itself and then forward again.

Piping with royal icing

Create elegant and detailed designs with royal icing, which can dry hard and hold its shape for 2D and 3D work. Colour as desired and use with dozens of different tips for varied effects. Piping is a skill really worth mastering, to achieve a truly professional finish.

Scrolls

Use a small shell or rope tip to create a series of interlinked scrolls for a border on a cake.

Rope

Use a rope tip to pipe a spring shape in a clockwise direction, using even pressure.

Filigree

This delicate piping work is created with a small writing tip and long piped lines of random patterns. Dust with lustre dust to highlight.

Beads and stringwork

Try small and large writing tips to create a finely piped line of beads. Link with loops of piped string work.

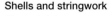

Shells and stringwork

Use a shell tip to create a row of symmetrical shapes, and then link them with piped stringwork, finishing off with a picot dot at the base of each shell.

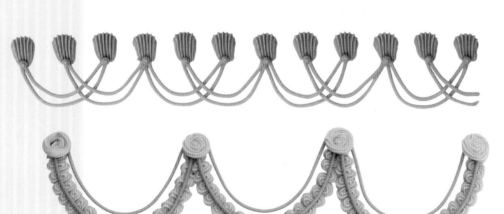

Ruffles and rosettes

A star tip creates a lovely rosette when turned in a clockwise motion. Link with a series of ruffles, using a small petal or open-star tip, and embellish with stringwork.

Shell border with stringwork

Use a shell tip to create a continuous shell border, and then a writing nozzle to pipe in diagonal lines for a lattice beneath.

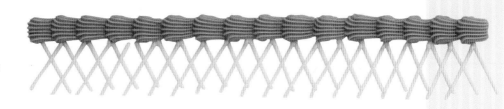

Star border

Create a star border in any size, with an open-star tip. Apply pressure until you get the required size, and then lift the bag upright for each shape.

Pulled beadwork

Use a slightly larger writing tip to create soft beads of icing and then drag them across to form a thinner tail.

Skein border

A skein is created with a small star tip, by piping in a clockwise direction at an even height to form the first curve and then pulling down in a point.

Zigzag ruffles

Use a small open star tip and pipe in a delicate back-and-forth motion to create the appearance of ruffles.

Swirls and picot dots

Use a fine writing tip to create elegantly piped curls, surrounding the larger swirls with a series of picot dots.

Damask 1

This ornate design can be created using a fine writing nozzle to pipe over a template or in the cut-out sections of a stencil.

Damask 2

To create this delicate pattern on the side of a cake, press a template onto the surface of the fondant and use a veining tool to emboss the shape for piping.

Trailing branches

Create fine and then slightly wider lines with a fine writing tip, and use the same tip for the beaded blossoms on the branches.

Piping with chocolate

You can pipe chocolate onto the surface of a cake, or allow the designs to harden in the fridge on a sheet of baking parchment, ready to affix later. Chocolate should be lukewarm to pipe effectively. Temper the chocolate (see p43) for the shiniest and hardest results.

- tracing paper or baking parchment template, optional
- piping bag with small, round decorating tip (such as Wilton no. 1L)

Ingredients

milk, white, or dark chocolate, melted and tempered (see p43)

1 Fill the piping bag with melted and tempered milk chocolate that has slightly cooled, so it is just warm. Fix a sheet of baking parchment on top of the template, and fix the sides with paper clips to hold it steady.

Tip

You can also pipe as you would with royal or buttercream icing, directly onto a cake. However, you may find it is easier to pipe onto a separate chocolate or fondant plaque, as you can wipe the piping off and start again if you make a mistake.

2 Press the tip against the surface of the baking parchment at the centre of the design and, working from the inside out, pipe lines over the template. Drag the tip along the paper, leaving a neat line of piping. Stop the pressure at the end of each line, and repeat, piping each line separately. Chill until hard.

Brushwork embroidery

Use royal icing to create beautiful, textured designs on a variety of cakes or decorations, with just a cutter and a paintbrush. This technique is called brushwork embroidery because the finished result is very much like a detailed, embroidered surface.

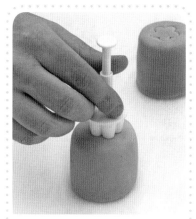

1 Lightly emboss an outline on the cake surface using a cutter. Allow the fondant to set for a few hours.

2 Fill the piping bag with royal icing. Working on one part of the design at a time, pipe over the embossed outline.

Ingredients

fondant-covered or smooth-iced cakes royal icing (coloured, if desired, see p39), thinned out with a little water

- cutter, to emboss
- piping bag with a narrow round piping tip

3 Dip a paintbrush in water, and draw it through the icing towards the centre of the design, using small, even strokes.

4 Continue to pull the icing into the centre of the design, until the shape is complete. Pipe more detail onto the design.

Tips
Keep the brush damp. You will be able to make 3 or 4 strokes before it needs to be dipped into water again. After the brushwork, pipe details, such as centres for flowers or stems for leaves, if desired. Allow to dry.

Painting a colour wash

Colour washes can highlight embossing, pick out textures on decorations, and provide a light background for further design work. You will need very diluted ready-made paint, or you can mix your own from colouring dust or paste and rejuvenator spirit.

Ingredients

edible liquid paint,
 colouring paste,
 or dusts in 2
 colours
rejuvenator spirit
 or vodka
embossed fondant-
 covered cake

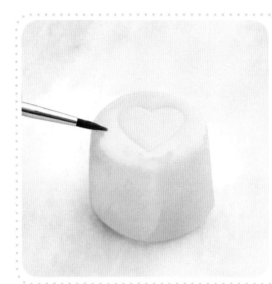

1 Dilute the paint with rejuvenator spirit to create a wash. Using a paintbrush, wash the paint over the embossed cake. You can cover evenly or unevenly, depending on the look you want. For a darker shade, colour wash the cake a second time and allow the excess paint to pool in the embossed grooves.

2 Paint some of the smaller areas or detailed sections of your embossed design, such as this heart, with another colour wash. You may wish to use a smaller brush for finer details like this. Allow to dry.

Variations

"Drag" by painting the surface with 1 colour, and gently brushing the cake in one direction and then the other using a clean, dry paintbrush. "Rag-roll" by using a balled-up piece of kitchen paper to apply and remove paint and create a mottled effect.

...provide a light background for further design work

Using sugar gems

Adorn your cakes with realistic edible jewels. Keep sugar gems, such as these sugar diamonds, in an airtight container and place them on the cake or decoration at the very last minute, or they will cloud. Use tweezers, rather than your fingers, to apply.

1 Dust a surface with cornflour and roll out the fondant to the desired thickness. Use a plunger cutter to cut out shapes, such as these daisies. Allow to dry until just beginning to harden.

Ingredients

cornflour, for dusting
strengthened fondant
    (see p52)
cupcakes piped with
    buttercream icing
royal icing (see p39)
large sugar
    diamonds

- **fondant roller**
- **large plunger**
    cutter
- **tweezers**

2 Moisten the back of each shape with water and apply to the top of your cake. Place a small amount of royal icing in the centre of each daisy, and top with a sugar diamond.

...place edible jewels on your cakes at the last minute

Strengthening fondant

Whether you choose to model fondant entirely by hand, or use cutters to create a variety of shapes, it is important to prepare the fondant so that it is pliable, strong, and able to dry hard enough. Use small quantities at a time, leaving the rest double-wrapped in cling film.

- fondant mat, marked with squares or diamonds
- fondant roller
- stitching (quilting) tool
- icing scraper or ruler to use for a straight edge
- 5cm (2in) circle cutter
- tweezers

Ingredients

white vegetable fat, for greasing
500g (1lb 2oz) fondant
2 tsp tylose powder

1 Lightly grease a flat surface and place the fondant on top. Knead the fondant until it is smooth. Make a well in the centre.

2 Place the tylose powder inside. Press the fondant around the well and knead the ingredients together.

3 When the fondant is smooth, pliable, and evenly coloured (with no streaks of strengthening powder), double-wrap it in cling film and place in a zip-lock bag to rest for 2 hours or overnight. You can omit this resting time, but it may lose some of its elasticity.

Tips
Always use "flower" grade or finely milled tylose powder to strengthen fondant. Coarser-milled powders are fine for making edible glue, but will make fondant lumpy and cause it to harden unevenly. Strengthen after colouring fondant, not before.

...pliable, strong, and able to dry hard enough for cutting and modelling

Crumb coating a cake

Crumb coating is like adding a base coat to a wall before painting. It helps to ensure a perfect finish for iced or fondant-covered cakes. It smoothes over any cracks or holes in the surface and helps the cake stay sealed and moist. You can crumb coat with buttercream or, if desired, ganache (see p30).

Ingredients

cakes, levelled, and layers filled with buttercream icing buttercream icing (see p38), thinned with some milk

• cake board
• turntable or lazy Susan

1 Place the cake on a board, or a turntable. Use a palette knife to carefully apply a thin layer of buttercream to the cake.

2 Start at the top of the cake, and swirl the buttercream over the surface as you turn it around on the turntable.

3 Spread the icing around the sides until evenly covered. A few crumbs may be embedded in the icing; this is normal.

4 Refrigerate or allow to dry – this can take up to 2 hours. Apply the final layer of icing or fondant.

...ensure a perfect finish for iced cakes

Crumb coating a cake

Stippling and sponging

These methods help you to create different textures on the surface of cakes or decorations. Use a stippling brush or specialized sponge to produce a subtle finish with tiny dots of colour. Sponging achieves a dappled result; try playing around with layers in different shades.

- stippling brush or sponge
- sponge

Ingredients

edible liquid paint,
  colouring paste,
  or dusts
rejuvenator spirit
  or vodka
fondant-covered or
  smooth-iced cakes

1 **To stipple**, lightly dip the stippling brush into edible liquid paint, heavily diluted with rejuvenator spirit.

2 Dot your brush on the surface of the cake in an up-and-down motion. Allow to dry and repeat, if desired.

Tips

Stipple, wash, or sponge shades of the same colour in layers to produce a textured look. Try sponging a lighter shade of a colour over a darker base, for the look of fabric. Dab the sponge heavily over some parts to look like velvet.

1 **To sponge**, you could use thicker paint for a bolder result. Dip the sponge into the paint and apply to the cake.

2 Rinse your sponge. Apply a second colour for a textured look. To avoid muddying, allow to dry before applying new colours.

...create different textures on the surface of cakes

Piping filigree with royal icing

Using a series of interlinked "W"s and "M"s, or simply long, continuous curls and lines, filigree is an elegant piping technique that you can use to create delicate, lace-like designs. Similar in approach, scrolled hearts can be piped on baking parchment and attached to the cake once dry.

1 Pipe an outline with the tip positioned just above the surface of the cake. Apply uniform, gentle pressure.

2 Pipe curves, bending continuously in all directions, but never touching. Do not lift the tip from the surface.

Ingredients

fondant-covered
  or royal-iced cake
  or cupcake
edible glue

• piping bag fitted with a small, very fine round tip (such as PME 00 or 0), filled with piping-consistency royal icing (see p39)
• template, optional

For scrolled hearts, use a template, if desired, to pipe a design onto a sheet of baking parchment. Dry until hard (overnight, if possible), carefully remove from the parchment, and affix them around the sides of your cake with a little edible glue.

Tips

For more intricate designs, you can use an icing "pen", which you fill with icing and use with one hand. The pen pushes the icing out without the need to squeeze. You can also purchase icing syringes, onto which you fit specialized tips.

Using icing sheets

Send an image to a specialist company and they can print it for you on icing sheets. To use, cut out and apply directly to the top of your cakes – or stick them onto rolled flower paste or strengthened fondant first. The sheets must be kept in an zip-locked bag or they will dry out.

Ingredients

printed icing sheet
cornflour, for dusting
strengthened fondant
   (see p52)
cupcakes piped
   with buttercream
   icing, optional

1 Carefully cut out all the images from the icing sheet with scissors and set aside. Dust a surface with cornflour and roll out the fondant to the desired thickness.

2 Moisten the surface of the fondant with a little water, using a pastry brush, and then arrange the images on top, as closely together as possible. Allow to dry for a few minutes and then cut out the images on the fondant, using a sharp knife.

Tips

You can wrap icing sheets with ready-printed patterns on them around the sides of your cake. Why not try leopard print for a handbag cake, or fairies and butterflies for a little girl's cake? The possiblities are endless.

...apply images to rolled, strengthened fondant

3 Place the images on a piece of baking parchment, image side up, and allow to dry overnight until hard.

4 Fix the images to piped cupcakes, if desired, by moistening the back of the fondant with water, using a pastry brush, and pressing into place.

Variation

You could print icing sheets yourself with lettering and/or images, but to do that you will need a specially adapted printer with edible ink. Alternatively, email your design to a specialist company who will print it for you.

Cupcakes and Muffins

Chocolate cupcakes

Children will enjoy decorating these – they can add their favourite sweets to the simple chocolate topping.

• serves 18–20

• prep 15 mins
• cook 18 mins

• standard bun tray
• standard cupcake
  cases

Ingredients

225g (8oz) unsalted butter,
   at room temperature
225g (8oz) caster sugar
225g (8oz) self-raising flour
1 tsp baking powder

4 eggs
2 tbsp cocoa powder
100g (3½oz) chocolate chips
175g (6oz) dark chocolate
flaked chocolate, to decorate

1 Preheat the oven to 180°C (350°F/Gas 4). Line a bun tray with 18–20 cupcake cases.

2 Place the butter, caster sugar, flour, baking powder, eggs, and cocoa powder in a large mixing bowl, and beat with a wooden spoon, electric hand whisk, or mixer until well combined. Stir in the chocolate chips, spoon the mixture into the cupcake cases, and bake for 18 minutes, or until well risen. Transfer to a wire rack to cool.

3 Melt the chocolate in a heatproof bowl over a pan of simmering water, then spoon over the top of the cooled cupcakes. Decorate with flaked chocolate. Leave until the chocolate has set.

Apple muffins

These are lovely served straight from the oven for breakfast.

• makes 12

• prep 10 mins
• cook 20–25 mins

• 12-cup muffin tin
• muffin cases

Ingredients

1 Golden Delicious apple,
  peeled and chopped
2 tsp lemon juice
115g (4oz) light demerara sugar,
  plus extra for sprinkling
200g (7oz) plain flour
85g (3oz) wholemeal flour

4 tsp baking powder
1 tbsp ground mixed spice
½ tsp salt
60g (2oz) pecan nuts, chopped
250ml (9fl oz) milk
4 tbsp sunflower oil
1 egg, beaten

1 Preheat the oven to 200°C (400°F/Gas 6). Line a 12-hole muffin tin with 12 muffin cases and set aside. Put the apple in a bowl, add the lemon juice, and toss. Add 4 tbsp of the sugar and set aside for 5 minutes.

2 Meanwhile, sift the plain and wholemeal flours, baking powder, mixed spice, and salt into a large bowl, tipping in any bran left in the sieve. Stir in the remaining sugar and pecans, then make a well in the centre of the dry ingredients.

3 Beat together the milk, oil, and egg, then add the apple. Tip the wet ingredients into the centre of the dry ingredients, and mix together lightly to make a lumpy batter.

4 Spoon the mixture into the paper cases, filling each case ¾ full. Bake the muffins for 20–25 minutes, or until the tops are peaked and brown. Transfer the muffins to a wire rack and sprinkle with extra sugar. Eat warm or cooled.

Cinnamon, apple, and sultana cupcakes

Apples and sultanas are an infallible combination and seem made for each other in these delicious, moist cupcakes.

- makes 12

- prep 15 mins
- cook 15 mins

- 12-hole cupcake tray
- paper cases
- piping bag and nozzle (optional)

Ingredients

115g (4oz) butter, at room temperature
115g (4oz) caster sugar
2 eggs
115g (4oz) self-raising flour
½ tsp baking powder
2 tsp ground cinnamon
3 green eating apples, peeled and grated, cores discarded
60g (2oz) sultanas

For the icing
225g (8oz) unsalted butter, at room temperature
450g (1lb) icing sugar, sifted
2 tbsp lemon juice
ground cinnamon, for dusting

1 Preheat the oven to 180°C (350°F/Gas 4). Line the tray with 12 paper cases.

2 Place the butter, sugar, eggs, flour, baking powder, and cinnamon in a large mixing bowl and beat well with a wooden spoon or electric whisk until light and fluffy. Add the grated apples and sultanas, and beat briefly again.

3 Spoon the mixture into the cases and bake for about 15 minutes or until well risen, golden, and the centres spring back when lightly pressed. Transfer to a wire rack to cool.

4 For the icing, beat the butter in a bowl. Gradually beat in the icing sugar and lemon juice until soft and fluffy. Pipe or spoon the icing on top of the cupcakes and dust with cinnamon.

Vanilla cupcakes

These pretty cupcakes are denser than fairy cakes, making it easier to decorate them with elaborate types of icing.

- makes 18–20

- prep 15 mins
- cook 20–25 mins

- 2 x 12-hole cupcake tray
- paper cases
- piping bag and star nozzle (optional)

Ingredients

200g (7oz) plain flour, sifted
2 tsp baking powder
200g (7oz) caster sugar
½ tsp salt
100g (3½oz) unsalted butter, at room temperature
3 eggs
150ml (5fl oz) milk
1 tsp vanilla extract

For the icing
200g (7oz) icing sugar
1 tsp vanilla extract
100g (3½oz) unsalted butter, at room temperature
4 tbsp natural food colouring (optional)
sprinkles, to decorate

1 Preheat the oven to 180°C (350°F/Gas 4) and place the flour, baking powder, caster sugar, salt, and butter in a bowl. Mix together with your fingertips until it resembles fine breadcrumbs.

2 In another bowl, whisk the eggs, milk, and vanilla extract together until well blended. Slowly pour the egg mixture into the dry ingredients, whisking all the time. Whisk gently until smooth, being careful not to over-mix, and then pour all the cake batter into a jug.

3 Line the tray with the paper cases and carefully pour the cake mixture into them, filling each one only half full. Bake in the preheated oven for 20–25 minutes until springy to the touch and a skewer inserted into the centre of a cupcake comes out clean. Leave for 2–3 minutes, then transfer the cupcakes to a wire rack to cool completely.

4 For the icing, combine the icing sugar, vanilla extract, butter, and food colouring (if using) in a bowl. Beat with an electric whisk for 5 minutes until very light and fluffy. Check the cupcakes have completely cooled, or they will melt the icing.

5 If icing by hand, add a teaspoonful of the icing mix to the top of each cake. Then, use the back of a spoon, dipped in warm water, to smooth the surface. For a more professional finish, transfer the icing to the piping bag and attach a star nozzle. Begin piping by squeezing out the icing with one hand, while holding the cake with the other. Start from the edge and pipe a spiral of icing that comes to a peak in the centre. Decorate each cake with a few sprinkles.

Banana and chocolate chip muffins

These moist muffins are perfectly sweet. If you can't find buttermilk, use the same quantity of plain yogurt instead.

• makes 8

• prep 15 mins
• cook 20–30 mins

• 12-hole muffin tin
• paper cases

• up to 12 weeks

Ingredients

100g (3½oz) plain flour
45g (1½oz) fine cornmeal
1 tsp baking powder
1 tsp bicarbonate of soda
100g (3½oz) golden sugar
45g (1½oz) butter, melted

1 medium egg, beaten
2 bananas, peeled and well mashed
85g (3oz) buttermilk
50g (1¾oz) milk chocolate, chopped
   into small chunks

1 Preheat the oven to 200°C (400°F/Gas 6). Line the tin with the paper cases and set aside.

2 In a large bowl, sift together the flour, cornmeal, baking powder, and bicarbonate of soda, then stir in the sugar. Set aside.

3 In a separate bowl, mix together the butter, egg, bananas, and buttermilk. Add the wet ingredients to the dry ingredients and fold together gently, taking care not to overmix. Fold in the chocolate chunks.

4 Divide the mixture between the muffin cases – it should fill them to just under the rims. Bake for about 20–30 minutes or until golden brown and firm to the touch. Remove from the oven and allow to cool in the tin.

Lime drizzle cupcakes

These are equally delicious made with a large lemon instead of the limes.

- makes 12

- prep 15 mins
- cook 15 mins

- 12-cup standard bun tray
- standard cupcake cases

Ingredients

115g (4oz) unsalted butter, at room temperature
115g (4oz) caster sugar
2 eggs
115g (4oz) self-raising flour
½ tsp baking powder
finely grated zest of 1 lime

For the topping
finely grated zest of 1 lime, or zest of 1 lime with ¾ finely grated, and ¼ thinly pared and cut into thin strips, to decorate (optional)
juice of 2 limes
55g (2oz) caster sugar

1 Preheat the oven to 180°C (350°F/Gas 4). Line the bun tray with 12 cupcake cases. Put the butter, sugar, eggs, flour, baking powder, and lime zest in a large mixing bowl. Beat well with a wooden spoon, electric hand whisk, or mixer until light and fluffy.

2 Spoon the mixture into the cupcake cases, and bake for about 15 minutes, or until well risen and the centres spring back when lightly pressed. Transfer to a wire rack to cool.

3 Meanwhile, boil the strips of lime zest in water for 2 minutes (if using), drain, rinse with cold water, drain again, and set side.

4 Mix the lime juice, grated zest, and sugar together. Prick the tops of the cakes lightly with a skewer and spoon a little of the mixture over each cake, catching any surplus syrup in a bowl underneath to drizzle again. Leave to set for a few seconds then repeat until all the drizzle is used. Decorate by coating the strips of lime zest (if using) with caster sugar and use to top each cupcake. Leave to cool. The lime juice will sink in leaving a lovely crusty top.

Blueberry and pistachio angel cupcakes

These cupcakes look beautiful and taste sublime, especially the sinfully smooth cream cheese icing.

• makes 12

• prep 25 mins
• cook 25 mins

• 12-hole cupcake tray
• paper cases

Ingredients

60g (2oz) shelled pistachio nuts
2 large egg whites
pinch of salt
½ tsp cream of tartar
115g (4oz) caster sugar
40g (1¼oz) plain flour
20g (¾oz) cornflour
¼ tsp natural almond extract

¼ tsp vanilla extract
85g (3oz) dried blueberries

For the cream cheese icing
150ml (5fl oz) double cream
4 tbsp icing sugar
140g (5oz) cream cheese
a few fresh or extra dried blueberries

1 Preheat the oven to 160°C (325°F/Gas 3). Line the tray with 12 paper cases.

2 Place the pistachios in a bowl, cover with boiling water and leave to stand for 5 minutes. Drain, then rub off the skins with a clean tea towel. Finely chop the pistachios and set aside half for decoration.

3 Place the egg whites in a dry, clean glass or metal bowl and lightly whisk with a balloon whisk or an electric whisk until foamy. Whisk in the salt and cream of tartar, and continue to whisk until the egg whites stand in stiff peaks.

4 Sift the sugar, flour, and cornflour over the egg whites, add the almond and vanilla extracts, the dried blueberries, and half the chopped nuts, then fold in gently with a metal spoon until just combined.

5 Spoon the mixture into the cases and bake for about 25 minutes or until risen, pale biscuit-coloured, and just firm to the touch. Transfer to a wire rack to cool.

6 For the icing, place the cream in a bowl and lightly whip with the icing sugar. Then whisk in the cream cheese until you have soft peaks. Spoon the icing over the cupcakes and decorate with the reserved pistachio nuts and a few fresh or dried blueberries.

Plum and almond friands

The almonds give these bite-sized cakes a rich flavour. Try fresh raspberries if you don't like plums.

• makes 16

• prep 15 mins
• cook 30–35 mins

• 6- and 12-hole
muffin tins
• paper cases

• up to 4 weeks

Ingredients

75g (2½oz) ground almonds
250g (9oz) icing sugar, sifted
75g (2½oz) plain flour, sifted

175g (6oz) butter, melted
6 large egg whites
9 small plums, stoned and quartered

1 Preheat the oven to 180°C (350°F/Gas 4). Line the tins with paper cases and set aside.

2 In a large bowl, mix together the almonds, icing sugar, flour, and butter. In another clean bowl, whisk the egg whites until stiff. Stir in a quarter of the egg whites into the almond mixture, then gently fold in the remainder.

3 Pour the mixture into the paper cases in the tins. Distribute the mixture equally – you may prefer to first pour the batter into a measuring jug, then use the jug measurements to carefully pour equal amounts into each case.

4 Divide the plums between the muffins, then place the larger tin on the top shelf of the oven, and the smaller tin on the middle shelf, and bake for about 20–25 minutes until lightly golden. Remove the larger tin and place the smaller one on the top shelf and bake for another 10 minutes or so. Cool for about 5–10 minutes in the tin, then remove and cool on a wire rack.

Orange and lemon cupcakes

Cupcakes that are easy to make, yet look very special. Choose your favourite colours and sprinkles to give them a personal touch.

• makes 12

• prep 15 mins
• cook 25–30 mins

• 12-hole cupcake tray
• paper cases
• piping bag and star nozzle (optional)

•up to 4 weeks, uniced

Ingredients

200g (7oz) butter, at room temperature
200g (7oz) golden granulated sugar
3 eggs, beaten
200g (7oz) plain flour, sifted
juice of 1 large orange

For the icing
50g (1¾oz) butter, at room temperature
125g (4½oz) icing sugar
juice of 1 lemon
a few drops of natural yellow food colouring (optional)
a few drops of natural orange food colouring (optional)
sprinkles, to decorate

1 Preheat the oven to 180°C (350°F/Gas 4). Line the tray with paper cases and set aside.

2 Whisk together the butter, sugar, eggs, and flour until pale and fluffy, then add the orange juice, a little at a time, until the mixture loosens its consistency and easily drops off the whisk.

3 Spoon the mixture into the cases evenly and bake in the oven for about 25–30 minutes or until lightly golden brown, risen, and springy to the touch. Leave to cool in the tin for 2–3 minutes before sitting them on the wire rack to cool completely.

4 For the icing, beat the butter and icing sugar together, then stir in the lemon juice. Divide the mixture into 2 bowls. If using the colouring, mix a few drops of each colour into the bowls of icing until it reaches the desired shade.

5 Ice by hand, using the back of a spoon dipped in warm water to smooth the surface, or transfer the icing to a piping bag and pipe onto the cupcakes (see p34). Decorate with sprinkles.

Chocolate muffins

The buttermilk brings a fantastic lightness to these muffins, which are sure to fix any chocolate cravings.

• makes 12

• prep 10 mins
• cook 15 mins

• 12-hole muffin tin
• paper cases

Ingredients

225g (8oz) plain flour
60g (2oz) cocoa powder
1 tbsp baking powder
pinch of salt
115g (4oz) soft light brown sugar

150g (5½oz) chocolate chips
250ml (9fl oz) buttermilk
6 tbsp sunflower oil
½ tsp vanilla extract
2 eggs

1 Preheat the oven to 200°C (400°F/Gas 6). Line the tin with the paper cases and set aside.

2 Sift the flour, cocoa powder, baking powder, and salt into a large bowl. Stir in the sugar and chocolate chips, then make a well in the centre of the dry ingredients.

3 Beat together the buttermilk, oil, vanilla extract, and eggs and pour the mixture into the centre of the dry ingredients. Mix together lightly to make a lumpy batter. Spoon the mixture into the paper cases, filling each three-quarters full.

4 Bake for 15 minutes or until well risen and firm to the touch. Immediately transfer the muffins to a wire rack and leave to cool.

Cherry and coconut cupcakes

This classic combination of flavours is always popular. If you like, the cakes can be coloured pink as well as the icing.

Ingredients

• makes 12–15

• prep 15 mins
• cook 15 mins

•15-hole cupcake tray
• paper cases
• piping bag and nozzle (optional)

115g (4oz) glacé cherries
115g (4oz) butter, at room temperature
115g (4oz) caster sugar
2 eggs
85g (3oz) self-raising flour
60g (2oz) desiccated coconut, plus extra for sprinkling
1½ tsp baking powder
a few drops of natural pink food colouring (optional)

For the icing
175g (6oz) butter, at room temperature
350g (12oz) icing sugar, sifted
4 tsp milk
a few drops of natural pink food colouring
25g (scant 1oz) desiccated coconut
12 glacé cherries

1 Preheat the oven to 180°C (350°F/Gas 4). Line the tray with 12–15 paper cases. Wash, dry, and quarter the cherries.

2 Place the butter, sugar, eggs, flour, coconut, and baking powder in a large mixing bowl and beat well with a wooden spoon or an electric whisk until light and fluffy. Add the quartered cherries. Add a few drops of pink food colouring (if using) and beat briefly again.

3 Spoon the mixture into the cases and bake for about 15 minutes or until well risen, golden, and the centres spring back when lightly pressed. Transfer to a wire rack to cool.

4 For the icing, beat the butter in a bowl. Gradually beat in the icing sugar and milk until soft and fluffy. Beat in a few drops of pink food colouring. Pipe or spoon the icing on top of the cupcakes and top each with a sprinkling of desiccated coconut and a glacé cherry.

Lemon and poppy seed muffins

Poppy seeds give these soft muffins an interesting texture – perfect for a summer snack.

• makes 12

• prep 10 mins
• cook 15 mins

• 12-hole muffin tin
• paper cases

Ingredients

250g (9oz) self-raising flour
1 tsp baking powder
¼ tsp salt
125g (4½oz) caster sugar
finely grated zest of 1 lemon
1 heaped tsp poppy seeds
100ml (3½fl oz) whole milk
100ml (3½fl oz) plain yogurt
3½ tbsp sunflower oil
1 large egg, beaten
2 tbsp lemon juice

For the glaze
2 tbsp lemon juice
150g (5½oz) icing sugar
finely grated zest of 1 lemon

1 Preheat the oven to 200°C (400°F/Gas 6) and line the tin with paper cases.

2 Sift the flour, baking powder, and salt into a large bowl. Using a balloon whisk, mix through the sugar, lemon zest, and poppy seeds.

3 Measure the milk, yogurt, and sunflower oil into a jug, then add the egg and lemon juice and beat it all together thoroughly.

4 Pour the liquid into the centre of the dry ingredients and mix with a wooden spoon until just combined. Be careful not to over-mix.

5 Divide the mixture between the paper cases equally and bake in the middle of the oven for 15 minutes until the muffins are lightly brown and well risen. Remove from the oven and allow them to cool in the tin for 5 minutes before transferring to a wire rack to cool completely.

6 When the muffins have cooled, mix the lemon juice and icing sugar together to form a thin icing, drizzle it in a zigzag pattern over the muffins, and sprinkle the tops with lemon zest.

Coffee walnut cupcakes

Walnuts lend a desirable crunch to these cupcakes, while the coffee icing is silky smooth and delicately flavoured.

• makes 12–15

• prep 15 mins
• cook 15 mins

• 15-hole cupcake tray
• paper cases
• piping bag and nozzle (optional)

❄

• up to 12 weeks

Ingredients

115g (4oz) butter, at room temperature
115g (4oz) caster sugar
115g (4oz) self-raising flour
½ tsp baking powder
2 eggs
2 tsp instant coffee granules, dissolved in 2 tsp hot water
85g (3oz) walnut halves, finely chopped

For the coffee icing
1 tbsp instant coffee granules, dissolved in 1 tbsp hot water
175g (6oz) butter, at room temperature
350g (12oz) icing sugar, sifted
12–15 walnut halves

1 Preheat the oven to 180°C (350°F/Gas 4). Line the tray with 12–15 paper cases.

2 Place the butter, caster sugar, flour, baking powder, eggs, and the coffee mixture in a large mixing bowl. Beat well with a wooden spoon or electric whisk until light and fluffy. Fold in the walnuts with a metal spoon.

3 Spoon the mixture into the cases and bake for about 15 minutes or until well risen, golden, and the centres spring back when lightly pressed. Transfer to a wire rack to cool.

4 For the icing, place the coffee mixture in a bowl. Beat in the butter and gradually add the icing sugar, beating until light and fluffy. Pipe or spoon the icing on top of the cooled cupcakes. Decorate each with a walnut half.

Blueberry muffins

If you don't like blueberries, try fresh raspberries, or orange zest instead of the lemon in these healthy muffins.

• makes 12

• prep 15 mins
• cook 20 mins

• 12-hole muffin tin
• paper cases

Ingredients

50g (1¾oz) butter
250g (9oz) self-raising flour
1 tsp baking powder
75g (2½oz) caster sugar
finely grated zest of 1 lemon (optional)

pinch of salt
250g (9oz) plain yogurt
2 large eggs, lightly beaten
250g (9oz) blueberries

1 Preheat the oven to 200°C (400°F/Gas 6). Line the tin with paper cases and set aside. Melt the butter in a small pan, then leave to cool. Sift the flour into a large bowl, mix in the baking powder, sugar, lemon zest (if using), and a pinch of salt, then make a well in the centre.

2 Mix the yogurt, eggs, and the cooled, melted butter together in a large jug, then pour into the dry ingredients, along with the blueberries. Mix until just combined, but try not to over-mix or the muffins will become heavy. The batter may be slightly lumpy.

3 Spoon the mixture evenly into the cases and bake for 20 minutes or until risen and golden. Cool in the tin for 5 minutes, then serve warm or leave to cool.

Berry friands

You could also use apricots, peaches, or plums instead of the berries in these juicy fruit muffins, but ensure they are ripe.

• makes 6

• prep 15 mins
• cook 30–35 mins

• 6-hole muffin tin
• paper cases

Ingredients

100g (3½oz) icing sugar
45g (1½oz) plain flour
75g (2½oz) ground almonds
3 large egg whites

75g (2½oz) unsalted butter, melted
150g (5½oz) mixed fresh berries,
    such as blueberries and raspberries

1 Preheat the oven to 180°C (350°F/Gas 4). Sift the icing sugar and flour into a bowl, then stir in the ground almonds. In another bowl, whisk the egg whites with an electric whisk until they form soft peaks.

2 Gently fold the flour mixture and the melted butter into the egg whites to make a smooth batter. Line the tin with paper cases and spoon the batter into them. Scatter over the berries, pressing them down slightly into the batter so they all fit in. Bake for 30–35 minutes or until golden brown and risen. Leave to cool in the tin.

Raspberry cupcakes

Elegant cupcakes that are a perfect partner for after-dinner coffee. The combination of fresh raspberries and white chocolate works splendidly.

• makes 18–20

• prep 15 mins
• cook 18 mins

• 2 x 12-hole cupcake trays
• paper cases

Ingredients

225g (8oz) unsalted butter, at room
   temperature
225g (8oz) caster sugar
225g (8oz) self-raising flour
1 tsp baking powder
4 eggs

3 tbsp ground almonds
150g (5½oz) raspberries,
   plus 18–20 extra, to decorate
175g (6oz) white chocolate,
   plus extra, grated, to decorate

1 Preheat the oven to 180°C (350°F/Gas 4). Line the trays with paper cases and set aside.

2 Place the butter, caster sugar, flour, baking powder, and eggs in a large mixing bowl and beat with an electric whisk for 2–3 minutes or until well combined. Stir in the ground almonds and raspberries, then spoon the mixture into the paper cases and bake for 18 minutes or until risen and golden brown. Place on a wire rack to cool completely.

3 Put the white chocolate in a bowl and place it over a pan of barely simmering water until the chocolate has melted. Drizzle over the top of the cupcakes. Decorate each one with grated white chocolate (see p29) and a raspberry.

Strawberry and cream cupcakes

These cupcakes are filled with a fresh strawberry filling and are a luscious treat for afternoon tea or pretty enough for a dessert.

- makes 12

- prep 15 mins
- cook 12 mins

- 12-hole cupcake tray
- paper cases
- piping bag and nozzle (optional)

Ingredients

2 eggs, separated
115g (4oz) caster sugar
85g (3oz) unsalted butter,
    at room temperature
85g (3oz) self-raising flour
30g (1oz) cornflour
½ tsp vanilla extract

For the filling and topping
225g (8oz) strawberries
30g (1oz) caster sugar
a few drops of lemon juice
150ml (5fl oz) double cream

1 Preheat the oven to 200°C (400°F/Gas 6). Line the tray with 12 paper cases.

2 Place the egg whites in a clean, dry glass or metal bowl and whisk until stiff, then whisk in 1 tablespoon of the sugar and set aside. In another bowl, beat the butter and sugar with a wooden spoon or an electric whisk until light and fluffy. Beat in the egg yolks. Sift the flour and cornflour over the surface, and beat in with 2 tablespoons of hot water and the vanilla extract. Gently fold in the whisked egg whites with a metal spoon. Do not over-mix, but make sure that the egg white is incorporated.

3 Spoon a heaped dessertspoon of the mixture into the cases and bake for about 12 minutes or until well risen, golden, and the centres spring back when lightly pressed. Transfer to a wire rack to cool.

4 For the filling and topping, select 6 small or 3 large strawberries, cut into halves or quarters, including their green hulls, and reserve for decoration. Hull and chop the remainder and sweeten to taste with a little of the sugar, and sharpen with a few drops of lemon juice. Whip the cream and the remaining sugar until peaking.

5 Cut out a circle of sponge from each cake so you end up with a small well in the centre, leaving a 5mm (¼in) border all round. Fill with the chopped strawberries. Pipe or spoon the whipped cream on top and place a strawberry half, or quarter, on top of each. Place the cut out rounds of sponge at a jaunty angle to the side of the strawberries and press gently into the cream to secure.

Lemon and blueberry muffins

These feather-light muffins are glazed with lemon juice for an extra burst of zesty tang, and are at their best served warm.

Ingredients

• makes 12

• prep 20–25 mins
• cook 15–20 mins

• 12-hole muffin tin
• paper cases

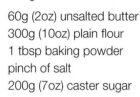

• up to 4 weeks

60g (2oz) unsalted butter
300g (10oz) plain flour
1 tbsp baking powder
pinch of salt
200g (7oz) caster sugar

1 egg
finely grated zest and juice of 1 lemon
1 tsp vanilla extract
250ml (9fl oz) milk
225g (8oz) blueberries

1 Preheat the oven to 220°C (425°F/Gas 7). Melt the butter in a pan over a medium-low heat. Sift the flour, baking powder, and salt into a bowl. Set 2 tablespoons sugar aside and stir the rest into the flour. Make a well in the centre.

2 In a separate bowl, beat the egg lightly until just broken down and mixed together. Add the melted butter, lemon zest, vanilla extract, and milk. Beat the egg mixture until foamy. In a slow, steady stream, pour the egg mixture into the well in the flour. Stir with a rubber spatula, gradually drawing in the dry ingredients to make a smooth batter. Gently fold in all the blueberries, taking care not to bruise any of the fruits. Do not over-mix, or the muffins will be tough. Stop when the ingredients are blended.

3 Line the tin with the paper cases. Spoon in the batter, filling to three-quarters full. Bake for 15–20 minutes or until a skewer inserted in the centre of the muffins comes out clean. Let the muffins cool slightly, then transfer them to a wire rack.

4 In a small bowl, stir the reserved sugar with the lemon juice until the sugar dissolves. While the muffins are warm, dip the crown of each into the sugar and lemon mixture. Set the muffins upright back on the wire rack and brush with any remaining glaze. The warm muffins will absorb the maximum amount of the lemony glaze.

Cupcakes and Muffins

Butterflies and blossoms

These charming cupcakes are spread with rich vanilla buttercream icing, topped with pretty pink fondant butterflies, and nestled in delicate lace cupcake wraps. Serve alongside delightful piped peach cupcakes with a simple yet elegant blossom on top.

- makes 18-20

- allow 1½ days including drying time

- fondant roller
- butterfly plunger
- cutters, medium and small
- blossom plunger cutter, medium
- piping bag with large open star tip (such as Wilton no. 1M)
- lace cupcake wrappers

Ingredients

200g (7oz) plain flour, sifted
2 tsp baking powder
200g (7oz) caster sugar
½ tsp salt
100g (3½oz) butter, at room temperature
3 eggs
150ml (5fl oz) milk
1 tsp vanilla extract

For the butterflies and blossom
cornflour, for dusting
200g (7oz) pink fondant, strengthened (see p52)
200g (7oz) white fondant, strengthened (see p52)

For the icing
1kg (2¼lb) buttercream icing (see p38), half coloured with peach colouring paste

1 A day before you wish to serve the cupcakes, on a flat surface dusted with cornflour, roll out the strengthened pink fondant to about 1mm (¹⁄₁₆in) thick. Use plunger cutters to cut out 10 medium and 10 small butterflies. Bend gently in the centre, and place along the crease of an open book lined with baking parchment to dry in shape overnight.Roll out the strengthened white fondant on a surface dusted with cornflour to about 1mm (¹⁄₁₆in) thick, and use the blossom plunger cutter to cut out 10 blossoms. Place on baking parchment to dry overnight.

2 To make the cupcakes, preheat the oven to 180°C (350°F/Gas 4). Place the flour, baking powder, caster sugar, salt, and butter in a bowl. Mix together with your fingertips until it resembles fine breadcrumbs. In another bowl, whisk the eggs, milk, and vanilla extract together until well blended. Slowly pour the egg mixture into the dry ingredients, whisking all the time. Whisk gently until smooth and then pour all the cake batter into a jug.

3 Line the tray with the paper cases and spoon a heaped dessertspoon of the mixture into the cases. Bake in the preheated oven for 20–25 minutes until springy to the touch. Leave for 2–3 minutes, then transfer the cupcakes to a wire rack to cool completely.

4 Using the cone method (see p35), fill the cooled cupcakes with buttercream icing. Using a palette knife, spread uncoloured buttercream icing on 6 cupcakes. Fill the piping bag with peach buttercream icing and attach the open star tip. Pipe the remaining cupcakes. Moisten the back of each fondant decoration and press gently onto the piped cupcakes.

Chocolate-frosted cupcakes

Kids will adore the creamy, chocolatey icing on these dainty cakes.

• makes 12

• prep 25 mins
• cook 20 mins

• 12-hole muffin tin
• muffin cases

• freeze, before icing, for up to 3 months

Ingredients

125g (4½oz) unsalted butter, at room temperature
125g (4½oz) caster sugar
2 large eggs, beaten
125g (4½oz) self-raising flour, sifted
1 tsp pure vanilla extract
1 tbsp milk, if necessary

For the icing
100g (3½oz) icing sugar
15g (½oz) cocoa powder
100g (3½oz) unsalted butter, softened
few drops of pure vanilla extract
25g (scant 1oz) milk chocolate or dark chocolate, shaved with a vegetable peeler

1 Preheat the oven to 190°C (375°F/Gas 5). Line the muffin tin with 12 muffin cases. Place the butter and sugar in a bowl, and cream together using a wooden spoon, an electric hand whisk, or mixer until pale and fluffy. Beat in the eggs a little at a time, adding a little of the flour each time. Add the vanilla extract, then the rest of the flour, and mix until smooth and combined – the mixture should drop easily off the spoon or beaters. If it doesn't, stir in the milk.

2 Divide the mixture between the muffin cases using two teaspoons. Bake for 20 minutes, or until risen, golden, and firm to the touch. Transfer the cupcakes to a wire rack to cool.

3 To make the icing, sift the icing sugar and cocoa powder into a bowl, add the butter and the vanilla extract, and whisk with an electric hand whisk until the mixture is light and fluffy. Spread the icing over the cupcakes, giving the top of each one a swirly design. Scatter the chocolate shavings over.

Cupcake bouquet

Pipe a medley of cupcakes to create buttercream roses, and arrange them in a ceramic flowerpot to create a delightful centrepiece for any occasion. You could choose a larger pot to feed a crowd. While piping can take time to master, the end result is well worth the effort.

Ingredients

12 cupcakes (see p96, steps 2 and 3)
100g (3½oz) buttercream icing
   see p38)
100g (3½oz) buttercream icing,
   coloured pale pink

100g (3½oz) buttercream icing,
   coloured fuchsia
25g (scant 1oz) royal icing
   (see p39)

1 When the cupcakes have cooled, fill each cake with a little buttercream icing, using a plain round piping or injector tip attached to a large piping bag.

2 Fix a large flower drop tip to the same piping bag, and pipe a rose on 4 cupcakes. Start from the centre of the cupcake and swirl outwards in an anticlockwise direction, using even pressure, until the entire surface of the cupcake is covered with a piped rose.

3 Wash the piping bag or fit the same tip to a new piping bag, and fill the bag with pale pink buttercream icing. Pipe 4 more cupcakes, using the same technique. Pipe the remaining cupcakes with fuchsia buttercream icing, in the same way. Allow the cupcakes to set for 5 minutes.

4 Place the polystyrene ball into the flowerpot and press 6 cocktail sticks into the surface, about 9cm (3½in) apart. Spread a little royal icing on the base of a cupcake case, and press it firmly onto a cocktail stick that has been inserted into the ball. Hold in place for 30 seconds, until the icing begins to dry. Repeat for the next cupcake in the same colour, and then attach 2 cupcakes of each colour.

5 Wrap the flowerpot with decorative ribbon tied into a pretty bow. Place the remaining cupcakes around the flowerpot.

- makes 12
- 1½ hrs
- large piping bag with injector tip, or plain round tip
- large flower drop tip (such as Wilton no. 2D)
- polystyrene ball, about 10cm (4in) wide
- ceramic flowerpot, about 12.5cm (5in) wide
- decorative ribbon

BRING IT ALL TOGETHER

Filling cupcakes
see p35

Piping a buttercream
rose *see p41*

Mini cakes and Cake pops

White chocolate cakes

These delicious cakes are studded with crunchy walnuts.

• makes 9

• prep 10 mins
• cook 30–35 mins

• 16cm (7in)
deep square
cake tin

Ingredients

50g (1¾oz) unsalted butter, at room
   temperature
50g (1¾oz) caster sugar
1 tsp pure vanilla extract
2 medium eggs, lightly beaten
100g (3½oz) self-raising flour
200g (7oz) white chocolate, finely chopped
100g (3½oz) walnuts, chopped

For the topping
200g (7oz) white chocolate
50g (1¾oz) walnuts, chopped, to
   decorate

1 Preheat the oven to 160°C (325°F/Gas 3). Grease the deep square tin with butter. Line with baking parchment and set it aside.

2 Cream the butter, sugar, and vanilla extract in a bowl with a wooden spoon or an electric hand whisk until pale and creamy. Add the eggs a little at a time, beating well after each addition. Gently fold in the flour, then the chocolate and the chopped walnuts.

3 Spread the mixture in the tin and smooth the top. Bake for 30–35 minutes, or until set. Cool in the tin for 10 minutes before turning out on to a wire rack to cool.

4 For the topping, melt the white chocolate in a heatproof bowl placed over gently simmering water, stirring, until smooth and glossy. Spread it evenly over the cooled cake. Allow it to set, then decorate with chopped walnuts, and cut it into 9 squares.

Chocolate fondants

Usually thought of as a restaurant dessert, chocolate fondants are actually surprisingly quick and easy to prepare at home.

• makes 4

• prep 20 mins
• cook 5–15 mins

• 4 x 150ml (5fl oz) dariole moulds, or 10cm (4in) ramekins

❄

• up to 1 week, unbaked

Ingredients

150g (5½oz) unsalted butter, diced, plus extra for greasing
1 heaped tbsp plain flour, plus extra for dusting

150g (5½oz) good-quality dark chocolate, broken into pieces
3 large eggs
75g (2½oz) caster sugar

1 Preheat the oven to 200°C (400°F/Gas 6). Thoroughly grease the sides and base of each dariole mould or ramekin. Dust the insides with a little flour, then turn the flour around in the dish until all the butter is covered with a thin layer of flour. Tip out the excess flour. Line the bases of the moulds with small discs of baking parchment.

2 Gently melt together the chocolate and butter in a heatproof bowl over simmering water, stirring occasionally. Make sure the base of the bowl does not touch the water. Cool slightly.

3 In a separate bowl, whisk together the eggs and sugar. Once the chocolate mixture has cooled slightly, beat it into the eggs and sugar until thoroughly combined. Sift the flour over the top of the mixture and gently fold it in.

4 Divide the mixture between the moulds, making sure that the mixture does not come right up to the top. At this stage, the fondants can be refrigerated for several hours or overnight, as long as they are brought back to room temperature before cooking.

5 Cook the fondants in the centre of the oven for 5–6 minutes if using moulds, or 12–15 minutes if using ramekins. The sides should be firm, but the centres soft to the touch. Run a sharp knife around the edge of the moulds or ramekins. Turn the fondants out onto individual serving plates by putting a plate on top and inverting the whole thing. Gently remove each mould or ramekin and peel off the parchment. Serve immediately.

Strawberries and cream whoopie pies

These strawberry layered whoopie pies make a charming addition to a traditional afternoon tea.

• makes 10

• prep 40 mins
• cook 12 mins

• up to 4 weeks, unfilled

Ingredients

175g (6oz) unsalted butter, at room temperature
150g (5½oz) soft light brown sugar
1 large egg
1 tsp vanilla extract
225g (8oz) self-raising flour
75g (2½oz) cocoa powder

1 tsp baking powder
150ml (5fl oz) whole milk
2 tbsp Greek yogurt or thick plain yogurt
150ml (5fl oz) double cream, whipped
250g (9oz) strawberries, thinly sliced
icing sugar, for dusting

1 Preheat the oven to 180°C (350°F/Gas 4). Line several baking sheets with parchment. Cream the butter and sugar until fluffy. Beat in the egg and vanilla extract. In a bowl, sift together the flour, cocoa, and baking powder. Mix the dry ingredients and the milk into the batter alternately, a spoonful at a time. Fold in the yogurt.

2 Put 20 heaped tablespoons of the batter onto the baking sheets, leaving space for the mixture to spread. Dip a tablespoon in warm water and use it to smooth over the surface of the pies.

3 Bake for 12 minutes until well risen. Leave the pies for 2–3 minutes, then turn out onto a wire rack to cool.

4 Spread the cream onto half the cakes. Top with a layer of strawberries and a second cake. Dust with icing sugar and serve.

Mini banana and chocolate topped cheesecakes

These dainty delights make superb petit fours to delight your guest at the end of a meal.

• makes 12

• prep 40 mins, plus chilling

• 12-hole muffin tin
• paper cases

• up to 4 weeks, no topping

Ingredients

125g (4½oz) all-butter shortbread
25g (scant 1oz) butter
100g (3½oz) white chocolate, broken into pieces
200g (7oz) cream cheese, at room temperature
2 large eggs, separated

100ml (3½fl oz) double cream
15g sachet of gelatine
50g (1¾oz) caster sugar
2 bananas
juice of half a lemon
50g (1¾oz) dark chocolate, grated, to decorate

1 Place the paper cases in the tin. Crush the shortbread biscuits – place them in a plastic bag and bash them with rolling pin until they are fine crumbs. Gently melt the butter in a small pan, then take off the heat and stir in the biscuit crumbs until well mixed. Divide the mixture evenly between the paper cases and press it in firmly, then chill in the refrigerator for about 30 minutes.

2 Melt the chocolate in a bowl set over a pan of simmering water, stirring occasionally. Set aside. In a large bowl, beat the cream cheese, egg yolks, and cream together until smooth, then stir in the melted chocolate.

3 Put 3 tablespoons of cold water into a small pan, sprinkle over the gelatine until absorbed, and heat very gently, swirling the liquid and stirring constantly; do not boil the water. As soon as the gelatine is dissolved, remove the pan from heat and stir the gelatine mixture into the cheesecake mix.

4 Whisk the egg whites together until stiff peaks form. Continue to whisk as you slowly incorporate the sugar. Fold this into the cheesecake mixture. Divide the mixture between the paper cases and put in the refrigerator to chill and set for at least 3 hours. Once set, remove the cheesecakes from the cases carefully, loosening them first with a cutlery knife. Slice the bananas and toss them in the lemon juice to prevent them from browning. Serve the cheesecakes topped with sliced banana and some grated chocolate (see p29).

Welsh cakes

Traditional small cakes from Wales that take minutes to prepare and cook, and you don't even have to remember to preheat the oven.

• makes 24

• prep 20 mins
• cook 16-24 mins

• 5cm (2in) pastry cutter
• large, heavy frying pan, cast iron skillet, or flat griddle

❄

• up to 4 weeks

Ingredients

200g (7oz) self-raising flour, plus extra for dusting
100g (3½oz) unsalted butter, chilled and diced, plus extra for frying
75g (2½oz) caster sugar, plus extra for sprinkling

75g (2½oz) sultanas
1 large egg, beaten
a little milk, if needed

1 Sift the flour into a large bowl. Rub the butter into the flour until the mixture resembles fine breadcrumbs. Mix in the sugar and the sultanas. Pour in the egg.

2 Mix the ingredients together, bringing the mixture into a ball using your hands. This should be firm enough to roll out, but if it seems too stiff add a little milk.

3 On a floured work surface, roll out the dough to about 5mm (¼in) thick and cut out disks, using the pastry cutter.

4 Heat the pan, skillet, or griddle over a medium-low heat. Fry the cakes, in batches, in a little melted butter for 2–3 minutes on each side until they puff up, are golden brown, and cooked through.

5 While still warm, generously sprinkle a little caster sugar over the cakes before serving. Welsh cakes are best eaten immediately.

Rock cakes

It's high time these British buns enjoyed a renaissance. Correctly cooked, they are incredibly light and crumbly.

• makes 12

• prep 15 mins
• cook 15–20 mins

• up to 4 weeks

Ingredients

200g (7oz) self-raising flour
pinch of salt
100g (3½oz) unsalted butter,
  chilled and diced
75g (2½oz) caster sugar

100g (3½oz) mixed dried fruit
  (such as raisins, sultanas, and
  mixed peel)
2 eggs
2 tbsp milk, plus extra if needed
½ tsp vanilla extract

1 Preheat the oven to 190°C (375°F/Gas 5). In a large bowl, rub together the flour, salt, and butter until the mixture resembles fine breadcrumbs. Mix in the sugar, then add the dried fruit and mix throughly.

2 In a jug, whisk together the eggs, milk, and vanilla extract. Make a well in the centre of the flour mixture and pour the egg mixture into it. Combine thoroughly to produce a firm mixture. Use a little more milk if the mixture seems too stiff.

3 Line 2 baking sheets with baking parchment. Place large heaped tablespoons of the mixture onto the baking sheets, leaving space for the cakes to spread. Bake in the centre of the oven for 15–20 minutes until golden brown. Remove to a wire rack to cool slightly. Split and serve warm.

Sticky walnut buns

A satisfying treat, these buns are great for lunchboxes or as an after-school snack for children.

• makes 12

• prep 15 mins
• cook 10-12 mins

• 12-hole non-stick cupcake tray

• up to 4 weeks, no topping

Ingredients

115g (4oz) butter, diced
175g (6oz) self-raising flour
60g (2oz) semolina or ground rice
85g (3oz) golden granulated sugar
115g (4oz) dates, finely chopped
60g (2oz) walnuts, chopped
2 large eggs, beaten
1 tsp vanilla extract

For the topping
1 tbsp coffee granules
115g (4oz) golden icing sugar
12 walnut halves, to decorate

1 Preheat the oven to 190°C (375°F/Gas 5). In a large bowl, rub the butter into the flour and mix well. Add the semolina or ground rice and combine.

2 Add the sugar, dates, and walnuts, mixing everything together. Pour in the eggs and vanilla extract and stir to a stiff consistency.

3 Divide the mixture equally between the 12 holes of the tray. Bake in the top of the oven for about 10–12 minutes. Remove from the oven and leave to cool.

4 For the topping, blend the coffee granules with 1 tablespoon of boiling water. Mix the coffee liquid with the icing sugar until it reaches drizzling consistency. Drizzle each drop with the coffee topping and decorate with half a walnut, then leave to set.

Fondant fancies

Dainty in size, gorgeous to look at, and delectable to eat, these little cakes are just the thing for a children's party.

• makes 16

• prep 20–25 mins
• cook 25 mins

• 20cm (8in) square cake tin
• paper cases

Ingredients

175g (6oz) unsalted butter, at room temperature, plus extra for greasing
175g (6oz) caster sugar
3 large eggs
1 tsp vanilla extract
175g (6oz) self-raising flour, sifted
2 tbsp milk
2–3 tbsp raspberry or red cherry conserve

For the buttercream
75g (2½oz) unsalted butter, at room temperature
150g (5½oz) icing sugar

For the icing
juice of ½ lemon
450g (1lb) icing sugar
1–2 drops natural pink food colouring
iced flowers, to decorate

1 Preheat the oven to 190°C (375°F/Gas 5). Grease the tin and line the base with baking parchment. Place the butter and sugar in a large bowl and beat until pale and fluffy. Set aside.

2 Lightly beat the eggs and vanilla extract in another large bowl. Add one-quarter of the egg mixture and a tablespoon of the flour to the butter mixture, and beat well. Add the rest of the egg mixture, a little at a time, beating as you go. Add the remaining flour and milk, and fold in.

3 Transfer the mixture to the tin and bake in the centre of the oven for about 25 minutes or until lightly golden and springy to the touch. Remove from the oven, leave to cool in the tin for about 10 minutes, remove from the tin and cool upside down on a wire rack. Remove the baking parchment.

4 For the buttercream, beat the butter with the icing sugar until smooth. Set aside. Slice the cake horizontally with a serrated knife and spread the fruit conserve on one half and the buttercream on the other. Sandwich the layers together, then cut the cake into 16 equal squares.

5 For the icing, put the lemon juice in a measuring jug and fill it up to 60ml (2fl oz) with hot water. Mix this with the icing sugar, stirring continuously and adding more hot water as required until the mixture is smooth. Add the pink food colouring and stir well.

6 Use a palette knife to transfer the cakes to a wire rack placed over a board or plate (to catch the drips). Drizzle with the icing to cover the cakes completely, or just cover the tops, and allow the icing to drip down the sides so the sponge layers are visible. Decorate with iced flowers, then leave to set for about 15 minutes. Use a clean palette knife to transfer each cake carefully to a paper case.

Sticky toffee puddings

A British classic, these puddings are ideal as individual desserts. The rich toffee sauce ensures just the right balance of sweetness.

• makes 8

• prep 20 mins
• cook 20–25 mins

• 8 x 200ml (7fl oz) pudding basins

• up to 8 weeks

Ingredients

125g (4½oz) unsalted butter, at room temperature, plus extra for greasing
200g (7oz) stoned dates (preferably Medjool)
1 tsp bicarbonate of soda
225g (8oz) self-raising flour
175g (6oz) dark or light soft brown sugar
3 large eggs

For the toffee sauce
150g (5½oz) dark or light soft brown sugar
75g (2½oz) unsalted butter, diced
150ml (5fl oz) double cream
pinch of salt
single cream, to serve

1 Preheat the oven to 190°C (375°F/Gas 5). Grease the pudding basins well, including all the corners.

2 In a small pan, simmer the dates with the bicarbonate of soda and 200ml (7fl oz) of water for 5 minutes until softened. Purée with the cooking liquid in a food processor or blender.

3 Sift the flour into a mixing bowl. Add the butter, sugar, and eggs, and mix with an electric whisk until well combined, then mix in the date purée. Pour the mixture into the pudding basins and place them on a baking tray.

4 Bake for 20–25 minutes or until firm to the touch. Meanwhile, make the toffee sauce. Heat the sugar, butter, and cream together in a pan, stirring occasionally, until the butter and sugar have melted and everything is smooth and combined. Stir in the salt and allow to boil for a 2–3 minutes. Serve the warm puddings with the hot toffee sauce and some single cream.

Strawberry shortcakes

The delicately sweetened strawberries in this classy dessert make it a light and fresh summer treat.

Ingredients

60g (2oz) unsalted butter,
   plus extra for greasing
250g (9oz) plain flour, sifted,
   plus extra for dusting
1 tbsp baking powder
½ tsp salt
45g (1½oz) caster sugar, plus extra
   for sprinkling
175ml (6fl oz) double cream,
   plus extra if needed

For the coulis
500g (1lb 2oz) strawberries, hulled
2–3 tbsp icing sugar
2 tbsp Kirsch (optional)

For the filling
500g (1lb 2oz) strawberries, hulled and sliced
45g (1½oz) caster sugar, plus 2–3 tbsp
250ml (9fl oz) double cream
1 tsp vanilla essence

1 Preheat the oven to 220°C (425°F/Gas 7) and grease a baking sheet. In a bowl, mix the flour, baking powder, salt, and sugar. Rub to form crumbs. Add the cream, tossing; add more, if dry. Add the butter and rub in with your fingertips to form crumbs.

2 Press the crumbs together to form a ball of dough. On a floured surface, lightly knead the dough. Pat out a round, 1cm (½in) thick, and cut out 6 rounds with the pastry cutter. Transfer to the baking sheet and bake for 12–15 minutes. Cool on a wire rack.

3 For the coulis, purée the strawberries, then stir in the icing sugar and Kirsch (if using).

4 For the filling, mix the strawberries and sugar. Whip the cream until soft peaks form (see p30). Add 2–3 tablespoons of sugar and the vanilla essence. Whip until stiff. Cut the cakes in half. Place the strawberries on the bottom halves, followed by the cream. Top each with its lid and sprinkle with caster sugar. Pour the coulis around and serve immediately.

Chocolate and vanilla whoopie pies

A modern classic, these versatile cake sandwiches are a sure-fire way to please a large crowd.

• makes 10

• prep 40 mins
• cook 12 mins

• up to 4 weeks, unfilled

Ingredients

175g (6oz) unsalted butter, at room temperature
150g (5½oz) soft light brown sugar
1 large egg
1 tsp vanilla extract
225g (8oz) self-raising flour
75g (2½oz) cocoa powder
1 tsp baking powder
150ml (5fl oz) whole milk
2 tbsp Greek yogurt or thick plain yogurt

For the vanilla buttercream and icing
100g (3½oz) unsalted butter, at room temperature
400g (14oz) icing sugar
2 tsp vanilla extract
2 tsp milk, plus extra if needed
white and dark chocolate, to decorate

1 Preheat the oven to 180°C (350°F/Gas 4). Line a few baking sheets with baking parchment. Cream together the butter and brown sugar until light and fluffy. Beat in the egg and vanilla extract to the creamed mixture. In a bowl, sift together the flour, cocoa, and baking powder. Gently fold a spoonful of the dry ingredients into the cake batter. Mix in a little of the milk. Repeat until all the milk and dry ingredients are combined. Fold in the yogurt.

2 Place 20 heaped tablespoons of mixture on the baking sheets, leaving space for the mixture to spread. Dip a tablespoon in warm water and use it to smooth the surface of the halves. Bake for around 12 minutes until a skewer inserted into the pies comes out clean. Cool on a wire rack.

3 For the buttercream filling, mix together the butter, half the icing sugar, and vanilla extract using a wooden spoon. Change to a whisk, and beat the mix for about 5 minutes until light and fluffy. If the mixture seems stiff, loosen with extra milk to make the icing spreadable.

4 Spread a tablespoon of the buttercream onto each of the flat sides of half the cakes. Sandwich together the iced with the uniced halves to form the pies, pressing gently.

5 To decorate, use a vegetable peeler to make white and dark chocolate shavings. Place the remaining icing sugar in a bowl and add 1–2 tablespoons of water to form a thick paste. Spoon the icing onto the top of each pie, spreading it out for an even covering. Lightly press the chocolate shavings onto the wet icing.

Mini cakes and Cake pops

Ball game mini cakes

Celebrate sport with some clever mini cakes, each adorned with a stencilled ball on top. You can top them with virtually any type of ball to please the crowds. Use an icing scraper to help remove excess icing when you are stencilling the cakes.

• makes 12

• 2½ hrs

• 12 x 5cm (2in)
  mini round
  cake tins
• fondant roller
• circle cutters,
15cm (6in) and 5cm
  (2in) diameter
• 12 x 7.5cm (3in)
round cake boards
• fondant smoother
• 3 x sports ball
  stencils
• 2m (6ft) black
ribbon, 1.5cm (⅝in)
  wide

Ingredients

175g (6oz) unsalted butter, softened
175g (6oz) caster sugar
3 eggs
225g (8oz) self-raising flour
grated zest of 1 lemon

For the icing
icing sugar, for dusting
2kg (4½lb) white fondant
tylose powder
100g (3½oz) royal icing (see p39), in black,
    red, and white
50g (1¾oz) orange fondant, strengthened
    (see p52)

1 Preheat the oven to 180°C (350°F/Gas 4). Whisk the butter and sugar until fluffy. Mix in the eggs one at a time. Whisk for 2 minutes more, until bubbles appear on the surface. Sift in the flour, add the zest, and fold in until just smooth.

2 Fill the mini cake tins with the same amount of mixture – roughly half to two-thirds full. Bake for 15–25 minutes until a skewer comes out clean. Allow the cakes to cool in the tins, then turn out onto a wire rack. Crumb coat with buttercream (see p53).

3 On a surface dusted with icing sugar, roll out the white fondant to 5mm (¼in) thick. Cut 12 circles using the large cutter. Use them to cover each cake. Trim off any excess. Dot a little buttercream icing on each cake board, and place the covered cakes on top. Shape the tops with the fondant smoother.

4 Strengthen the remaining white fondant with tylose powder (see p52), and roll it to 3mm (⅛in) thick. Use a knife to cut out 8 squares, 6cm (2¼in) in size. Place the football stencil on one and spread black royal icing over the top. Peel off the stencil and repeat on 3 more squares. Stencil 4 baseballs using the red royal icing. Cut out 4 squares from orange fondant rolled to the same thickness, and stencil white icing basketballs on top.

5 Use the smaller cutter to cut a disc around each ball. Dab each cake with a little water, and carefully place a design on each. Trim the cakes with ribbon, secured with royal icing.

Wedding mini cakes

Iced with ganache, wrapped in chocolate fondant and finished off with a pretty ribbon and chocolate roses, these gorgeous miniature wedding cakes make an ideal favour or sophisticated dessert. For completely edible cakes, cut your ribbons from white-chocolate modelling clay instead.

Ingredients

175g (6oz) unsalted butter, softened
175g (6oz) soft light brown sugar
3 eggs
125g (4½oz) self-raising flour
50g (1¾oz) cocoa powder
1 tsp baking powder
2 tbsp Greek yogurt
chocolate buttercream icing (see p38)

For the icing
1.2kg (2¾lb) dark chocolate fondant
tylose powder
900g (2lb) dark chocolate ganache
　(see p30)
icing sugar, for dusting
50g (1¾oz) dark chocolate, melted
edible glue

• serves 12

• allow 1½ days, including drying time

• 12 x 5cm (2in) mini round cake tins
• fondant roller
• small rose leaf plunger cutter
• scraper, smooth-edged
• fondant smoother
• 2.5m (8ft) ivory grosgrain ribbon, 12mm (½in) wide

1 Preheat the oven to 190°C (375°F/Gas 5). Whisk the butter and sugar until fluffy. Mix in the eggs one at a time. In a separate bowl, sift together all of the dry ingredients. Fold the flour mixture into the batter, until well blended. When the batter is fluffy, gently fold through the yogurt.

2 Fill the mini cake tins with the same amount of mixture – roughly half to two-thirds full. Bake for 15–25 minutes until a skewer comes out clean. Allow the cakes to cool in the tins, then turn out onto a wire rack. When cool, halve and fill with chocolate buttercream.

3 Strengthen 200g (7oz) of the dark chocolate fondant with tylose powder (see p52) and allow to rest overnight. When the fondant is pliable, hand-model 12 small roses (see p11), 2.5cm (1in) wide. Set aside to dry for about 30 minutes. Roll out more strengthened fondant to 2mm (¹⁄₁₆in) thick and use the rose leaf plunger cutter to cut out 24 leaves. Curve the tips, and leave to dry for about 30 minutes. Use a palette knife to spread the sides and top of each cake with ganache. Run the icing scraper over the surface.

4 On a surface dusted with icing sugar, roll out the remaining dark chocolate fondant to 3mm (⅛in) thick. Cut out 12 circles that are large enough to cover each cake, and smooth the fondant down over the cakes with a fondant smoother. Trim off any excess from the base, and allow to rest for 30 minutes.

5 Use the melted chocolate to fix a rose and 2 leaves to the top of each cake. Cut the ribbon into 12 equal lengths, and wrap around the base of each cake, fixing the join with edible glue.

Teddy bear mini cakes

These colourful cakes are layered with fondant and flower paste, and piped to create building blocks – perfect for a baby shower, or a birthday celebration. The shade of the coloured royal icing will deepen with time, so aim for one shade lighter.

• makes 10

• allow 1½ hours

• 40 x 28cm oblong cake tin or mini cake tins, greased and floured, to make 10 cakes
• fondant roller
• square cutters: 7cm (2¾in), and 5cm (2in)
• fondant smoother
• mini bear cutter
• piping bag with tips (such as PME no. 1 and no. 5)

Ingredients

200g (7oz) unsalted butter, softened
200g (7oz) caster sugar
4 large eggs
1 tsp vanilla extract
200g (7oz) self-raising flour, sifted
1 tsp baking powder
100g (4oz) vanilla buttercream icing

For the decoration

1.5kg (3lb 3oz) white fondant
cornflour, for dusting
200g (7oz) each orange, lilac, blue, green, and pink fondant
edible glue
200g (7oz) royal icing, for piping (see p39)
black, orange, lilac, blue, green, and pink colouring paste

1 Preheat the oven to 180°C (350°F/Gas 4). Whisk the butter and sugar until fluffy. Mix in the eggs one at a time. Stir in the vanilla and beat until bubbles appear on the surface. Using a metal spoon, fold in the flour and baking powder until combined. Spoon into the tin and bake for 25–30 minutes until a skewer comes out clean. Cool on a wire rack for at least 2 hours, and crumb coat with buttercream icing (see p53).

2 Knead the white fondant and roll out on a corn flour-dusted surface, to about 3mm thick. Cut 10 squares large enough to cover the cakes. Lay one on each cake and smooth down the sides with a fondant smoother. Trim off the excess and set for 30 minutes.

3 Roll out the orange fondant to about 2mm thick and cut out 10 squares with large cutter and then cut out the centre of each with the smaller cutter to create a frame. Cut out 4 teddy shapes and put all to one side to dry. Repeat with the lilac, blue, green and pink fondant. Moisten the backs of the frames and apply to the sides and tops of the cakes, smoothing the joins. Roll 20 tiny balls of white fondant with your fingers, and press into small circles. Moisten the backs and fix to create teddy snouts. Fit a no. 1 nozzle to a small piping bag and fill with a little black royal icing. Carefully pipe eyes, nose, ears and mouth detail onto each teddy.

4 Divide the remaining royal icing between 5 bowls and use food-colouring paste to achieve a colour that is as close as possible to the fondant shades. Attach a no. 5 tip to a piping bag and fill with coloured royal icing. Pipe a number or a letter on two sides and the top of each cake, then fill the inside. Moisten the backs of the bears and fix to the remaining two sides of each cake.

Tip

If you are not confident at piping freehand, you can use letter and number cutters to emboss the surface of the squares and pipe to fill later on. Alternatively, cut them out from the appropriate fondant, and fix them in place with edible glue.

Chocolate fudge cake balls

These must-have cakes are deceptively simple to make. Packet or leftover cake can also be used to save time.

• makes 20–25

• prep 35 mins, plus chilling
• cook 25 mins

• 18cm (7in) round cake tin

• up to 4 weeks, undipped

Ingredients

100g (3½oz) unsalted butter, at room temperature, or soft margarine, plus extra for greasing
100g (3½oz) caster sugar
2 eggs
85g (3oz) self-raising flour
20g (¾oz) cocoa powder
1 tsp baking powder
1 tbsp milk, plus extra if needed

250g (9oz) dark chocolate cake covering
50g (1¾oz) white chocolate

For the icing
125g (4½oz) unsalted butter
25g (scant 1oz) cocoa powder
125g (4½oz) icing sugar
2 tbsp milk, if needed

1 Preheat the oven to 180°C (350°F/Gas 4). Grease the tin and line with baking parchment. Cream the butter and sugar with an electric whisk until fluffy. Beat in the eggs, one at a time, mixing well between additions, until smooth and creamy.

2 Sift together the flour, cocoa, and baking powder, and fold into the cake batter. Mix in enough milk to loosen the batter to a dropping consistency. Spoon into the tin and bake for 25 minutes until the surface is springy to the touch and a skewer entered into the centre comes out clean. Cool on a wire rack. Whizz the cake in a food processor until it looks like breadcrumbs. Place 300g (10oz) in a bowl.

3 For the icing, melt the butter over a low heat. Stir in the cocoa powder and cook gently for 1–2 minutes, then leave to cool completely. Sift the icing sugar into a bowl and add the melted butter and cocoa. Beat together to combine. If a little dry, add the milk, 1 tablespoon at a time, until the icing is smooth and glossy. Leave to cool for up to 30 minutes. It will thicken as it cools.

4 Add the icing to the cake crumbs and blend together to make a smooth, uniform mix. Using dry hands, roll the cake mix into balls, each the size of a walnut. Put the balls on a plate and refrigerate for 3 hours or freeze for 30 minutes until firm.

5 Line 2 trays with baking parchment. Melt the cake covering according to packet directions and coat the balls in chocolate. Work quickly and if they start to break up, coat one at a time. Using 2 forks, turn the balls in the chocolate until covered. Remove, allowing excess to drip. Transfer the coated cake balls to the trays to dry. Melt the white chocolate in a bowl placed over a pan of boiling water. Drizzle the white chocolate over the balls with a spoon, to decorate. Leave the white chocolate to dry completely before transferring to a serving plate.

Mini cakes and Cake pops

White chocolate and coconut snowballs

With a marvellously refined look, these coconut balls are sophisticated enough to offer to guests as sweet canapés.

• makes 25–30

• prep 40 mins,
  plus chilling
• cook 25 mins

• 18cm (7in) round
  cake tin

❄

• up to 4 weeks,
  undipped

Ingredients

100g (3½oz) unsalted butter, at room
  temperature, or soft margarine,
  plus extra for greasing
100g (3½oz) caster sugar
2 eggs
100g (3½oz) self-raising flour
1 tsp baking powder
225g (8oz) desiccated coconut
250g (9oz) white chocolate cake covering

For the icing
100g (3½oz) unsalted butter, at room
  temperature
200g (7oz) icing sugar
2 tsp vanilla extract
2 tsp milk, plus extra if needed

1 Preheat the oven to 180°C (350°F/Gas 4). Grease the tin and line the base with baking parchment. Cream the butter or margarine, and sugar until pale and fluffy. Beat in the eggs, one at a time, beating well between each addition. Sift together the flour and baking powder, and fold into the cake batter.

2 Pour the batter into the tin and bake for 25 minutes. Turn out onto a wire rack to cool and remove the baking parchment. When the cake is cool, blend in a food processor until it resembles fine breadcrumbs. Place 300g (10oz) in a bowl.

3 For the icing, mix together the butter, icing sugar, and vanilla with a wooden spoon. Then whisk for about 5 minutes until light and fluffy. If the mixture seems stiff, loosen with milk.

4 Add the icing and 75g (2½oz) of the desiccated coconut to the cake crumbs, and mix together. With dry hands, roll the mix into balls the size of a walnut. Refrigerate for 3 hours or freeze for 30 minutes. Line 2 trays with baking parchment and put the remaining coconut on a plate.

5 Melt the chocolate cake covering in a heatproof bowl over a pan of barely simmering water. Place the chilled cake balls, one at a time, into the melted chocolate mixture, using 2 forks to turn them until covered. Transfer them to the plate of coconut. Roll them around in the coconut, then transfer to the baking tray to dry. You will have to work fast, as the chocolate can harden quickly, and the balls start to disintegrate if they are left in the chocolate too long.

Bridal lace cupcakes

These cupcakes have royal icing filigree and a piped snail's trail painted with pearl lustre dust. Ideal as wedding favours or a sweet treat to accompany a cake, they provide the perfect finishing touch for a special day. Measure the surface of your cupcakes first, to ensure that the fondant circles will cover the top exactly.

• makes 12

• 2 hours

• fondant roller
• circle cutter,
about 7.5cm (3in)
in diameter
• small piping bag
• fine piping tips
(such as PME no. 1
and 2)

Ingredients

icing sugar, for dusting
200g (7oz) white fondant
12 cupcakes (see p66), lightly iced with
    buttercream icing (see p38)

150g (5½oz) royal icing, for piping (see p39)
edible pearl lustre dust
rejuvenator spirit or vodka
12 edible diamonds

1 On a surface dusted with icing sugar, roll out the white fondant to about 3mm (⅛in) thick and use the cutter to cut out 12 circles. Moisten the backs of the circles with a little water and place them on top of the cupcakes, smoothing them until flat.

2 Fit a no. 1 tip to a small piping bag and fill with royal icing. Pipe the surface of each cupcake with delicate filigree (see p55). Leave a border of about 2mm (¹⁄₁₆in) around the outside of each fondant circle.

3 Fit a no. 2 tip to the piping bag and pipe delicate beading around the outside of the fondant circle (see p42). Allow to dry for 1 hour, or until hard.

4 Mix together some edible pearl lustre dust with rejuvenator spirit, and carefully paint the piped border. Place a dot of royal icing in the centre of each cupcake and place an edible diamond on top.

Wedding cake pops

A delightful way to add shimmery elegance to your wedding party, these cake pops can also be wrapped up for guests to take home – or elegantly displayed to form a centrepiece for each table!

Ingredients

48 cake-pop balls (see pp36–37)
400g (16oz) ivory candy melts or white chocolate, melted
150g (3oz) pink candy melts, melted
tylose powder
25g (1oz) ruby red fondant

25g (1oz) green fondant
25g (1oz) white fondant
50g (2oz) royal icing
pearl-white lustre dust
rejuvenator spirit

• makes 48

• allow 1 day

• 48 cake-pop sticks
• fondant roller
• blossom plunger cutter (small)
• piping bag and no. 00 tip
• paintbrush
• ribbon to decorate

1 Insert sticks into all of the cake balls and allow to set for 30 minutes. When cool and firm, dip 36 balls into the melted ivory or white chocolate, and place upright. Dip the remaining balls into the pink melts.

2 Knead a little tylose powder into both green and red fondant and allow to rest for 15 minutes. Use the red fondant to form roses, first creating tiny cones, and then forming small ovals with your fingers, moistening the base and wrapping them round the cone until you have a series of petals, and then gently pull down the edges. Allow to set.

3 Roll out the green fondant and use a sharp knife to cut 16 tiny leaves. Use the back of a knife to score the veins. Allow to set for 30 minutes and then use a little royal icing to fix leaves and rose to the pops.

4 Roll out the white fondant very thinly and cut 32 flowers with the plunger cutter. Moisten the backs with water and press onto the pink pops.

5 Fill a piping bag with royal icing, and pipe tiny dots over the surface of each pink pop. On the remaining ivory pops, pipe a series of beads in a cross across, by squeezing and then dragging your tip. Pipe tiny dots in the space around. Leave for 2 hours to dry.

6 Mix together the rejuvenator fluid with the lustre dust, and paint the beaded cake pops in long, even strokes, until they are fully covered. Attach the ribbons and display!

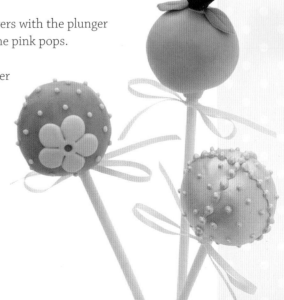

Christmas cake pops

Guaranteed to bring a smile, these delightful Christmas cake pops are a lovely way to offer a sweet treat or party favour with minimum fuss. Use dabbed water to fix on your fondant decorations.

• makes 16
(8 of each design)

• allow ½ day,
including drying
time

• 16 cake-pop
sticks
• fondant roller
• small piping bag
with fine tip (such
as PME no. 1)
• ribbon to
decorate

Ingredients

50g (1¾oz) brown flower paste
25g (1oz) each orange, brown, black, and white fondant, strengthened (see p52)
16 un-dipped cake pops, stick inserted (see pp36–37)
400g (14oz) white chocolate melts, melted
200g (7oz) milk chocolate melts, melted

100g (3½oz) red fondant, strengthened (see p52)
50g (1¾oz) royal icing, for piping (see p39)
edible white petal dust
edible pink petal dust
50g (1¾oz) green fondant
edible black pen

1 Make 16 antlers with pea-sized balls of brown flower paste. Roll into 4cm (1½in) sticks with pointed ends. Knead the orange fondant into 8 carrots, shaping peppercorn-size pieces into cones and scoring the surface. Allow the shapes to dry.

2 Dip half the cake pops in melted white chocolate melts and press the carrot noses into the surface while soft. Dip the rest in the melted milk chocolate melts and press the antlers into the surface. Set the pops upright, to harden.

3 Use the brown and red fondant to decorate the reindeer. Score the smile with a piping tip, and use white and black fondant for the eyes, adding a piped royal icing gleam.

4 Dust the snowmen with edible white petal dust and a little edible pink petal dust for the cheeks. Use red and green fondant to model hats and the holly. Roll tiny balls of black fondant for the eyes. Create a smile with the edible black pen. To finish, wrap a length of ribbon around each cake pop.

Scary cake pops

These festive lantern, spooky black cat, and witch's hat cake pops are the ideal treats for a Halloween party. Make a few batches to delight trick-or-treaters, and stand them upright for a striking centrepiece. When modelling your shapes, be sure to wrap excess fondant in cling film for future use.

Ingredients

25g (scant 1oz) yellow fondant
green colouring paste
tylose powder
cornflour, for dusting
100g (3½oz) black fondant, strengthened (see p52)
24 un-dipped cake pops on sticks (see pp36–37), 8 formed into cones with a flat base (for hats), and 8 with vertical ridges (for pumpkins)
400g (14oz) black candy melts
200g (7oz) orange candy melts
25g (scant 1oz) pink fondant
edible felt-tip black pen

• makes 24

• allow 1 day, including drying time

• fondant roller circle cutter, 5cm (2in)
• 24 cake-pop sticks

1 Colour a little yellow fondant with green colouring paste, strengthen (see p52), and mould into 8 stalks. Roll out the black fondant, use the cutter to cut 8 circles. Poke a central hole through each and place on scrunched foil. Allow all shapes to dry overnight.

2 Dip the hat (cone) and cat (round) cake pops in melted black candy melts and set aside, upright, to harden. Dip the pumpkins in melted orange melts and top with the stalks.

3 Roll out the remaining black fondant. Cut out the pumpkin features, triangles for the cats' ears, and strips to wrap around the hats. Allow to dry for 20 minutes. Use the yellow and pink fondant to create features for the cats, adding details to the cats' eyes with edible pen. Fix all of the cat and pumpkin features onto the pops with a little water.

4 Moisten the black circles, and slide them onto the hat cake-pop sticks. Moisten the black strips and fix to each hat.

Pirate cake pops

Create the perfect pirate party atmosphere with these yummy, easy-to-make cake pops – a great way to use up leftover fondant.

Ingredients

24 cake-pop balls (see pp36–37)
150g (6oz) melted peach candy melts
150g (6oz) melted green candy melts
50g (2oz) red fondant
50g (2oz) blue fondant
tylose powder

25g (1oz) yellow fondant
10g (½oz) white fondant
Scraps of black fondant
2 tbsp royal icing, white
2 tbsp royal icing, black

• makes 24

• allow 1 day, including drying time

• 24 cake-pop sticks
• fondant roller
• small circular cutters
• paintbrush
• small piping bag
• piping nozzle

1 Attach the cake-pop sticks to the balls, and once firm, dip 12 of the cake-pop balls into melted peach candy covering. Allow to dry upright. Use your hands to mould the remaining 12 cake pops into parrot bodies. Dip into the melted green candy covering and allow to set.

2 Roll out the red fondant very thinly and cut four small red circles. Moisten the backs and drape over 4 of the peach cake pops to form a bandana. Do the same with the blue fondant on 4 peach cake pops.

3 Knead a little tylose powder to the remaining red and blue fondant, and the yellow, white and black fondant. Form bandana ties with pinched triangles of red and blue fondant and fix to the bandanas. Mould the yellow fondant into 4 parrot beaks and set to one side to harden slightly.

4 Roll thin ropes of red, yellow and blue fondant, and stick them together with a little water. Flatten slightly with the roller and cut 8 wings for the parrots. Moisten the back and fix to the body, along with the beaks. Roll 8 tiny balls of white fondant, flatten, and fix to the head for eyes.

5 Roll out the black fondant very thinly and create 8 eye patches for the pirates and fix with a little water.

6 Fill the piping bag with white royal icing and carefully pipe dots onto the bandanas. Next, fill a piping bag with black icing and carefully pipe the pirates' mouths, and the parrot and pirates' eyes. Allow to dry for 30 minutes before displaying.

Princess cake pops

A princess party will never be complete without these stunning cake pops, which can be easily wrapped and sent home as party favours! Make them as glittery as you can! They couldn't be easier!

Ingredients

24 cake-pop balls (see pp36–37)
200g (8oz) melted pink candy melts
200g (8oz) melted pale green candy melts
25g (1oz) fuchsia fondant

4 tbsp royal icing, pink
4 tbsp royal icing, white
shimmer-pink lustre dust
glitter dust

• makes 24

• allow 1 day, including drying time

• 24 cake-pop sticks
• fondant roller
• tiny heart cutter
• piping bag and no. 00 tip
• ribbon to decorate

1 While the cake-pop balls are still warm, mould 12 of them into a heart shape and pop into the freezer to set for 30–40 minutes. Insert your cake-pop sticks, allow to harden in place, and then dip into the melted pink candy covering. Dry upright for 30 to 60 minutes.

2 Insert sticks into the remaining balls and dip into the melted green covering. Dry upright.

3 While drying, roll out the fuchsia fondant very thinly on a dusted surface and cut out about 120 small hearts. Moisten the backs, and then fix to the surface of the green cake pops.

4 Blend a pinch of pink lustre dust into the pink royal icing, and fill a bag with a small tip. Pipe tiny dots on the surface of the heart-shaped pops. Use a new bag to pipe white dots of royal icing. While still moist, sprinkle a very fine layer of glitter dust over all of the cake pops. Allow to set and tie with a pretty ribbon.

Mini bakes and Slices

Double chocolate brownies

Proving that two types of chocolate are always better than one, these brownies are rich, moist, and toothsome.

• makes 16

• prep 20 mins
• cook 30 mins

• 23cm (9in) square
cake tin or
25 x 15cm (10 x 6in)
cake tin

• freeze for
up to 3 months

Ingredients

300g (10oz) 70 per cent dark chocolate, chopped
125g (4½oz) unsalted butter, at room temperature
200g (7oz) light soft brown sugar
75ml (2½fl oz) olive oil

3 medium eggs, beaten
1 tsp pure vanilla extract
75g (2½oz) plain flour
25g (scant 1oz) cocoa powder
½ tsp baking powder
175g (6oz) white chocolate, chopped

1 Preheat the oven to 180°C (350°F/Gas 4) and grease the baking tin.

2 Place 200g (7oz) of the dark chocolate and the butter in a heatproof bowl, set it over a saucepan of simmering water, and stir occasionally until melted.

3 Place the butter and chocolate mixture, sugar, olive oil, eggs, and vanilla extract in a large bowl and mix with a wooden spoon until combined. Sift over the flour, cocoa powder, and baking powder, and fold in gently with a metal spoon. Then fold in the white chocolate and the remaining dark chocolate.

4 Transfer the mixture to the prepared tin and bake for 25–30 minutes, or until set on top and a skewer inserted into the centre comes out with some moist crumbs attached. Remove from the oven and leave to cool completely in the tin, then remove from the tin and cut into 16 pieces.

Prepare ahead
The brownies will keep for up to 5 days in an airtight container.

White chocolate and macadamia nut blondies

A white chocolate version of the ever-popular brownie.

• makes 24

• prep 25 mins
• cook 20 mins

• 22 x 30cm
(8¾ x 12in)
rectangular
cake tin

Ingredients

300g (10oz) white chocolate, chopped
175g (6oz) unsalted butter, cubed
300g (10oz) caster sugar
4 large eggs

225g (8oz) plain flour
100g (3½oz) macadamia nuts,
    roughly chopped

1 Preheat the oven to 200°C (400°F/Gas 6). Line the base and sides of the tin with baking parchment. In a bowl set over a pan of simmering water, melt the chocolate and butter together, stirring now and again until smooth. Remove, and leave to cool for about 20 minutes.

2 Once the chocolate has melted, mix in the sugar (the mixture may well become thick and grainy, but the eggs will loosen the mixture). Using a balloon whisk, stir in the eggs one at a time, making sure each is well mixed in before you add the next. Sift in the flour, fold it in, and then stir in the nuts.

3 Pour the mixture into the tin and gently spread it out into the corners. Bake for 20 minutes, or until just firm to the touch on top but still soft underneath. Leave to cool completely in the tin, then cut into 24 squares, or rectangles, for bigger blondies.

Toffee brownies

These attractively decorated brownies would be perfect for a children's party.

- makes 18

- prep 20 mins
- cook 40-45 mins

- 28 x 18cm
(11 x 7in) shallow
cake tin

- freeze for
up to 3 months

Ingredients

100g (3½oz) dark chocolate, broken into
  pieces, plus 50g (1¾oz) extra, to
  decorate
175g (6oz) unsalted butter
350g (12oz) caster sugar
4 large eggs

2 tsp pure vanilla extract
200g (7oz) plain flour
1 tsp baking powder
100g (3½oz) pecans, roughly chopped
200g (7oz) creamy toffees
75ml (2½fl oz) double cream

1 Preheat the oven to 180°C (350°F/Gas 4). Line the base of the baking tray with baking parchment.

2 Place the chocolate in a large heatproof bowl with the butter. Set the bowl over a saucepan of simmering water and stir occasionally until the chocolate has melted and the butter is well combined. Remove from the heat, then stir the sugar into the melted chocolate mixture.

3 Lightly beat the eggs with the vanilla in another bowl, then stir them into the chocolate mixture. Sift the flour and baking powder into the mixture, fold in lightly with a metal spoon, then fold in the pecans.

4 Place the toffees and cream in a saucepan over a gentle heat and stir continuously until melted.

5 Transfer half the chocolate mixture to the baking tin and spoon ½ of the toffee sauce over. Spread the rest of the chocolate mixture on top and bake for 40–45 minutes, or until firm to the touch. Remove from the oven, leave to cool in the tin for 20 minutes, then turn out. Remove the baking parchment, then transfer to a wire rack to cool completely.

6 Decorate by reheating the remaining toffee sauce. Place the extra chocolate in a small heatproof bowl, set the bowl over a saucepan of simmering water, and stir until the chocolate has melted. Drizzle the toffee sauce over the brownie, followed by the melted chocolate, using the tip of a teaspoon. Leave to cool, then cut into 18 pieces.

Prepare ahead
The brownies will keep in an airtight container for up to 5 days.

Flapjacks

These chewy bars are simple to make, using only a few storecupboard ingredients.

• serves 16–20

• prep 15 mins
• cook 40 mins

• 25cm (10in)
square cake tin

Ingredients

225g (8oz) unsalted butter, plus extra
    for greasing
225g (8oz) light soft brown sugar

2 tbsp golden syrup
350g (12oz) rolled oats

1 Preheat the oven to 150°C (300°F/Gas 2). Lightly grease the square cake tin.

2 Put the butter, sugar, and syrup in a large saucepan, and heat over a medium-low heat until the butter has melted. Remove the pan from the heat, and stir in the oats.

3 Transfer the mixture to the prepared tin, and press down firmly. Bake for 40 minutes, or until evenly golden and just beginning to brown at the edges.

4 Leave to cool for 10 minutes, then cut into 16 squares, or 20 rectangles. Leave in the tin until completely cooled.

Prepare ahead
These will keep for a few days in an airtight container.

Sticky date flapjacks

These flapjacks with a gooey layer of dates are ideal for lunch boxes.

• serves 16

• prep 25 mins
• cook 40 mins

• 20cm (8in)
square cake tin
• blender

Ingredients

200g (7oz) stoned dates
   (medjool are best), chopped
½ tsp bicarbonate of soda
200g (7oz) unsalted butter

200g (7oz) light soft brown sugar
2 tbsp golden syrup
300g (10oz) rolled oats

1 Preheat the oven to 160°C (325°F/Gas 3). Line the square cake tin with baking parchment. Place the dates and bicarbonate of soda in a pan with enough water to cover, simmer for 5 minutes, then drain, reserving the liquid. Whiz to a purée in a blender with 3 tbsp cooking liquid, then set aside.

2 Melt the butter, sugar, and syrup together in a large pan, stirring until the mixture forms a smooth sauce (you might need to give it a quick whisk to bring it together). Stir in the oats, then press half the mixture into the base of the tin.

3 Spread the date purée over the top of the oats, then spoon the remaining oat mixture over the top, gently easing it over the dates. Bake for 40 minutes, or until golden brown. Leave to cool in the tin for 10 minutes, then mark into 16 squares. Leave to cool completely in the tin, before cutting and serving.

Mocha slices

A whisper of coffee flavour suffuses the rich topping on this shortbread slice.

Ingredients

300g (10oz) all-butter shortbread
  biscuits
150g (5½oz) unsalted butter
100g (3½oz) dark chocolate,
  broken into small pieces

100g (3½oz) coffee-flavoured chocolate,
  broken into small pieces
3 large eggs
75g (2½oz) caster sugar
1 tbsp cocoa powder

• makes 8

• prep 20 mins
• cook 15–20 mins

• 20 x 30cm
(8 x 12in)
rectangular
shallow
loose-bottomed
tart tin

1 Preheat the oven to 190°C (375°F/Gas 5). Grease the tart tin and line with baking parchment.

2 Place the shortbread in a large plastic bag and seal. Hit the bag with the side of a rolling pin until the biscuits are crushed into crumbs. Melt half the butter in a medium-sized saucepan, then remove from the heat, and add the crushed biscuits. Stir well, until the crumbs are completely coated in the butter, then spread the mixture on to the base of the prepared tin, pressing it firmly into the edges of the tin. Set aside.

3 Melt the dark and coffee-flavoured chocolate with the remaining butter in a small heatproof bowl set over a pan of simmering water, stirring occasionally. Then remove the bowl and set aside to cool slightly.

4 In a large bowl, whisk together the eggs and sugar with a balloon whisk or an electric hand whisk for about 5–8 minutes, until thick and creamy, then fold in the melted chocolate. Pour the mixture over the biscuit base. Bake for about 10–15 minutes, until the top forms a crust. Remove and leave to cool completely in the tin. Sprinkle with cocoa powder, and slice into 8 rectangular slices to serve.

Good with
Pouring cream and fresh cherries or raspberries.

Cherry flapjacks

These upmarket flapjacks have the perfect texture, and the oats give them a delicious toasty flavour.

• makes 18

• prep 20 mins,
  plus chilling
• cook 25 mins

• 20cm (8in) square
  shallow cake tin

Ingredients

150g (5½oz) unsalted butter
75g (2½oz) light soft brown sugar
2 tbsp golden syrup
350g (12oz) rolled oats
125g (4½oz) glacé cherries, quartered, or

75g (2½oz) dried cherries, roughly
  chopped
50g (1¾oz) raisins
100g (3½oz) milk or white chocolate,
  broken into small pieces, to decorate

1 Preheat the oven to 180°C (350°F/Gas 4). Lightly grease the cake tin.

2 Place the butter, sugar, and syrup in a medium saucepan over a low heat, and stir until the butter and sugar have melted. Remove the saucepan from the heat, add the oats, cherries, and raisins, and stir until well mixed. Transfer the mixture to the prepared tin and press down.

3 Bake at the top of the oven for 25 minutes. Remove from the oven, allow to cool slightly in the tin, then mark into 18 pieces with a knife.

4 When the block of flapjacks is cold, place the chocolate in a small heatproof bowl, set it over a saucepan of simmering water, and stir occasionally until the chocolate has melted. Drizzle the melted chocolate over the flapjacks using a teaspoon, then chill for about 10 minutes, or until the chocolate has set.

5 Remove the block of flapjacks from the tin and cut into pieces as marked.

Prepare ahead
The flapjacks can be kept in an airtight container for up to 1 week.

Florentine slices

Cut into slices, these yummy treats are an easy-to-make great variation on traditional round Florentines.

• makes 16

• prep 20 mins
• cook 40–45 mins

• 20cm (8in) square
shallow cake tin

Ingredients

225g (8oz) plain chocolate,
  broken into pieces
60g (2oz) unsalted butter
115g (4oz) demerara sugar
1 egg, beaten

60g (2oz) mixed dried fruit
115g (4oz) desiccated coconut
60g (2oz) chopped mixed peel
  or glacé cherries

1 Grease the cake tin and line with baking parchment.

2 Place the chocolate in a small heatproof bowl, set it over a saucepan of simmering water, and stir occasionally until the chocolate has melted. Spoon the melted chocolate into the prepared cake tin, and spread it evenly over the base. Chill in the refrigerator to set while you make the Florentine mixture.

3 Preheat the oven to 150°C (300°F/Gas 2). Place the butter and sugar in a large bowl and cream together using a wooden spoon or an electric hand whisk until light and fluffy. Beat in the egg.

4 Mix the remaining ingredients in a separate bowl, then add them to the butter mixture. Stir well to ensure the fruit is evenly distributed, then spoon the mixture over the set chocolate in the tin.

5 Bake in the centre of the oven for 40–45 minutes, or until golden brown. Remove from the oven and leave to stand in the tin for 5 minutes.

6 Mark out 16 squares using a sharp knife, but make sure you do not cut into the chocolate – it is still runny and if your knife touches it, the sides of the squares will be smeared with chocolate. Leave until completely cold, then cut right through, loosen each square with a knife, and remove carefully from the tin.

Prepare ahead
The slices can be stored in an airtight container for up to 1 week.

Mini bakes and Slices

Panforte

This famous cake from Siena, Italy, dates from the 13th century.

• serves 12–16

• prep 30 mins
• cook 30 mins

• 20cm (8in)
loose-bottomed
cake tin

Ingredients

rice paper, for lining
115g (4oz) whole blanched almonds,
　toasted and roughly chopped
125g (4½oz) hazelnuts,
　toasted and roughly chopped
200g (7oz) mixed candied orange and
　lemon peel, chopped
115g (4oz) dried figs, roughly chopped
finely grated zest of 1 lemon

½ tsp ground cinnamon
½ tsp freshly grated nutmeg
¼ tsp ground cloves
¼ tsp ground allspice
75g (2½oz) rice flour or plain flour
30g (1oz) unsalted butter
140g (5oz) caster sugar
4 tbsp clear honey
icing sugar, to dust

1 Preheat the oven to 180°C (350°F/Gas 4). Line the base and sides of the cake tin with greaseproof paper, then put a disc of rice paper on top of the paper.

2 Put the almonds, hazelnuts, candied peel, figs, lemon zest, cinnamon, nutmeg, cloves, allspice, and flour in a large bowl, and mix well.

3 Put the butter, caster sugar, and honey in a pan, and heat gently until melted. Pour into the fruit and nut mixture, and stir to combine. Spoon into the prepared tin and, with damp hands, press down to create a smooth, even layer.

4 Bake for 30 minutes, then remove from the oven, leaving it in the tin to cool and become firm. When completely cold, remove the panforte from the tin. Peel off the paper, but leave the rice paper stuck to the bottom of the cake.

5 Dust heavily with icing sugar, and serve cut into small wedges.

Prepare ahead
This can be stored in an airtight container for up to three days.

Raspberry, lemon, and almond bake

Sweet almond cake topped with tart raspberries is a moreish treat.

• serves 8

• prep 20 mins
• cook 35–40 mins

• 20cm (8in) square
loose-bottomed
cake tin

• freeze for
up to 2 months

Ingredients

125g (4½oz) plain flour
1 tsp baking powder
75g (2½oz) ground almonds
150g (5½oz) unsalted butter, cubed
200g (7oz) caster sugar

juice of 1 lemon (about 3 tbsp)
1 tsp pure vanilla extract
2 large eggs
200g (7oz) fresh raspberries, chopped
icing sugar, to dust (optional)

1 Preheat the oven to 180°C (350°F/Gas 4). Line the base and sides of the cake tin with baking parchment. Sift the flour into a bowl, add the baking powder and ground almonds, and mix well. In a pan, melt the butter, sugar, and lemon juice together, stirring until well combined.

2 Stir this syrupy mixture into the dry ingredients, then mix in the vanilla extract and the eggs, one at a time, until the mixture is smooth and well combined. Pour into the tin, then scatter the raspberries over the top. Bake for 35–40 minutes, or until golden, and a skewer inserted into the cake comes out clean.

3 Cool in the tin for 10 minutes, then turn out and cool completely on a wire rack. Dust with icing sugar before serving (if using). To serve, cut into rectangles.

Toffee apple traybake

Bake this on a winter evening and serve warm for a special treat.

• makes 18
squares

• prep 20 mins
• cook 45 mins

• 22 x 30cm
(8¾ x 12in)
rectangular
cake tin

Ingredients

350g (12oz) Bramley apples, peeled,
   cored, and thinly sliced
squeeze of lemon juice
350g (12oz) self-raising flour
2 tsp baking powder
350g (12oz) light soft brown sugar
4 large eggs, lightly beaten
225g (8oz) unsalted butter, melted
1 tbsp caster sugar

For the toffee sauce
100g (3½oz) unsalted butter
100g (3½oz) light soft brown sugar
1 tbsp lemon juice
salt

1 Preheat the oven to 180°C (350°F/Gas 4). Line the base and sides of the tin with baking parchment. Put the apple slices in a bowl, and toss with the lemon juice to stop them turning brown while you make the cake mixture.

2 Sift the flour into a large mixing bowl, add the baking powder and brown sugar, and stir well. Mix in the eggs and the melted butter to make a smooth batter. Pour into the tin and smooth the top. Arrange the apple slices in three or four long lines along the top of the mixture, and sprinkle with the caster sugar. Bake for 45 minutes, or until the cake is firm to the touch, and a skewer inserted into the middle comes out clean.

3 Meanwhile, make the sauce by melting the butter, sugar, and lemon juice in a pan with a pinch of salt, whisking with a balloon whisk or electric hand whisk until the mixture is thick, melted, and smooth. Leave to cool slightly. Pour the sauce over the cake while it is still in the tin, gently brushing the sauce all over the top of the cake. Serve warm or cold.

Good with
A spoonful of crème fraîche.

Chocolate and hazelnut brownies

A classic American recipe, these brownies are moist and squidgy in the centre and crisp on top. The dusting of cocoa adds a slight bitterness.

• makes 24 squares

• prep 25 mins
• cook 17–20 mins

• 23 x 30cm (9 x 12in) brownie tin

Ingredients

100g (3½oz) hazelnuts
175g (6oz) unsalted butter, diced
300g (10oz) good-quality dark chocolate, broken into pieces
300g (10oz) caster sugar

4 large eggs, beaten
200g (7oz) plain flour
25g (scant 1oz) cocoa powder, plus extra for dusting

1 Preheat the oven to 200°C (400°F/Gas 6). Scatter the hazelnuts over a baking tray. Toast the nuts in the oven for 5 minutes until browned, being careful not to burn them. Remove from the oven and rub the hazelnuts in a dry, clean tea towel to remove the skins. Chop the hazelnuts roughly – some big chunks and some small, and set aside.

2 Line the base and sides of the tin with baking parchment and allow some of it to hang over the sides. Place the butter and chocolate in a heatproof bowl over a pan of simmering water, and melt, stirring until smooth. Remove from the heat and leave to cool. Once the mixture has cooled, mix in the sugar until well blended. Add the eggs, a little at a time, being careful to mix well between additions.

3 Sift in the flour and cocoa powder, lifting the sieve up above the bowl to aerate. Fold in the flour and cocoa until the batter is smooth and no patches of flour can be seen. Stir in the chopped nuts to distribute them evenly in the batter; the batter should be thick. Pour into the prepared tin and spread so the mixture fills the corners. Smooth the top. Bake for 12–15 minutes or until just firm to the touch on top and still soft underneath. A skewer inserted should come out coated with a little batter. Remove from the oven.

4 Leave the brownie to cool completely in the tin to maintain the soft centre. Lift the brownie from the tin using the edges of the parchment to get a good grip. Using a long, sharp, or serrated knife, score the surface of the brownie into 24 even pieces. Boil a kettle, and pour the boiling water into a shallow dish. Keep the dish close at hand. Cut the brownie into 24, wiping the knife between cuts and dipping it in the hot water. Sift cocoa powder over the brownies.

Apricot crumble shortbread

You can make the fruity topping in the food processor – use the pulse button so the mixture isn't overworked.

- makes 10 bars, or 20 squares

- prep 20 mins, plus chilling
- cook 1 hr 15 mins

- 12.5 x 35.5cm (5¼ x 14¼in) tin

Ingredients

200g (7oz) unsalted butter,
   at room temperature
100g (3½oz) caster sugar
200g (7oz) plain flour
100g (3½oz) cornflour
400g can apricots in natural juice,
   drained and roughly chopped

For the topping
75g (2½oz) butter, diced
150g (5½oz) plain flour
75g (2½oz) demerara sugar
   or caster sugar

1 Line the tin with baking parchment. Cream the butter and sugar together in a bowl with an electric whisk until pale and creamy. Sift in the flour and cornflour, and combine so that the mix comes together to form a dough. You'll probably need to use your hands to bring it together at the end. Knead the dough lightly until smooth, then push evenly into the base of the tin and smooth the top. Chill in the refrigerator for at least an hour or until firm.

2 Preheat the oven to 180°C (350°F/Gas 4). Make the topping by rubbing the butter into the flour in a bowl with your fingertips until the mixture resembles breadcrumbs. Stir in the sugar. Scatter the apricots evenly over the chilled base, then top with the buttery crumb mixture, pressing down quite firmly.

3 Bake for 1¼ hours or until a skewer inserted into the centre comes out clean with no uncooked mixture on it (it might be a bit damp from the fruit, though). Leave to cool in the tin. When cold, remove from the tin and cut into 10 bars or 20 squares.

Triple chocolate crunch bars

A delightful mix of three types of chocolate, these dark treats are perfect for any sweet craving. Use just your favourite type of chocolate if you prefer.

- makes 9 rectangles

- prep 10 mins
- cook 20–25 mins

- 15 x 25cm (6 x 10in) tin

Ingredients

250g (9oz) butter, at room temperature, plus extra for greasing
200g (7oz) caster sugar
3 medium eggs, beaten
200g (7oz) self-raising flour

50g (1¾oz) cocoa powder, plus extra for dusting
50g (1¾oz) dark chocolate, chopped
50g (1¾oz) milk chocolate, chopped
50g (1¾oz) white chocolate, chopped

1 Preheat the oven to 200°C (400°F/Gas Mark 6). Grease the tin with butter and line with baking parchment.

2 Cream the butter and sugar in a bowl using an electric whisk until smooth and creamy. Add the beaten eggs, a little at a time, beating continuously.

3 Fold in the flour, cocoa powder, and all the chocolate, and spread into the prepared tin.

4 Bake for 20–25 minutes until the sides have set and the centre is still a little sticky. Remove, cover with foil, and allow to cool. Dust with cocoa powder and cut into 9 rectangles to serve.

Coffee kisses

These delicate, little sandwiched hearts, with a subtle but aromatic coffee flavour, are a real crowd pleaser.

• makes 18

• prep 20–25 mins
• cook 10–15 mins

• 4cm (1½in) heart-shaped cookie cutter

• up to 12 weeks, uniced

Ingredients

75g (2½oz) butter
175g (6oz) self-raising flour
2 tsp custard powder
50g (1¾oz) caster sugar
1 medium egg yolk
2 tsp strong instant coffee (or 4 tsp, for a stronger coffee flavour), dissolved in 4 tsp hot water

For the buttercream
50g (1¾oz) unsalted butter, at room temperature
100g (3½oz) icing sugar
2 tsp espresso, or strong coffee made with water

1 Preheat the oven to 180°C (350°F/Gas 4). In a large bowl, rub the butter into the flour, then mix in the custard powder and sugar. Add the egg yolk and coffee and mix to a stiff paste. Knead to bring everything together.

2 Roll out the mixture between 2 sheets of cling film to a thickness of about 3mm (⅛in). Use a 4cm (1½in) heart-shaped cutter to cut out 36 heart shapes.

3 Place on 1 large baking tray or 2 medium sized baking trays, and bake for 10–15 minutes until golden. Cool on the tray for 5 minutes, then place on a wire rack to cool completely.

4 In a medium-sized bowl, cream together the buttercream ingredients. Use a spoon or palette knife to spread the buttercream on 1 biscuit half and sandwich it together with another half. Repeat with all the remaining biscuit halves.

Good with
A spoonful of crème fraîche.

Chocolate and toffee shortbread

Shortbread becomes utterly addictive once topped with rich chocolate and sticky toffee.

• makes 24

• prep 20 mins, plus chilling
• cook 45–50 mins

• 20cm (8in) square shallow loose-bottomed cake tin

Ingredients

250g (9oz) unsalted butter, at room temperature
175g (6oz) golden granulated sugar
225g (8oz) plain flour
125g (4½oz) semolina

4–5 tbsp ready-made toffee sauce
150g (5½oz) dark chocolate, broken into pieces
150g (5½oz) white chocolate, broken into pieces

1 Preheat the oven to 150°C (300°F/Gas 2). Lightly grease the tin and line with baking parchment. Whisk the butter and sugar together until pale and creamy, then add the flour and semolina and mix until well combined. Press the mixture into the tin and level the surface with a knife.

2 Bake in the oven for 40–45 minutes or until lightly golden, then remove and leave it to cool. Spoon the toffee sauce evenly over the shortbread and smooth the surface with the back of a spoon until level.

3 In 2 separate heatproof bowls, each set over a pan of simmering water, melt the dark and white chocolate, making sure the bowl does not touch the water. Spoon the dark and white chocolate randomly over the toffee sauce layer, and create a marbled effect by blending them slightly with the end of a teaspoon. Chill for 1–2 hours for the chocolate to set. Remove from the tin, place on a chopping board, and cut into 24 small squares with a large knife.

Sour cherry and chocolate brownies

The sharp flavour and chewy texture of the dried sour cherries contrast wonderfully with the rich, dark chocolate.

Ingredients

150g (5½oz) unsalted butter, diced, plus extra for greasing
150g (5½oz) good-quality dark chocolate, broken into pieces
250g (9oz) soft light brown muscovado sugar

3 eggs
1 tsp vanilla extract
150g (5½oz) self-raising flour, sifted
100g (3½oz) dried sour cherries
100g (3½oz) dark chocolate chunks

• makes 16 squares

• prep 15 mins
• cook 20–25 mins

• 20 x 25cm
(8 x 10in)
brownie tin

1 Preheat the oven to 180°C (350°F/Gas 4). Grease the tin and line with baking parchment. Melt the butter and chocolate in a heatproof bowl over a small amount of simmering water. Remove from the heat, add the sugar, and stir well to combine thoroughly. Cool slightly.

2 Mix the eggs and vanilla extract into the chocolate mixture. Pour the wet mix into the sifted flour and fold together, being careful not to over-mix. Fold in the sour cherries and chocolate chunks.

3 Pour the brownie mixture into the tin and bake in the centre of the oven for 20–25 minutes. They are ready when the edges are firm, but the middle is soft to the touch.

4 Leave to cool in the tin for 5 minutes. Turn out and cut into 16 squares. Place the brownies onto a wire rack to cool.

Raspberry flapjacks

Full of crunchy coconut, wholesome oats, and juicy raspberries, these flapjacks make a healthy snack on the go.

- makes 18 rectangles

- prep 10 mins
- cook 25 mins

- 15 x 25cm (6 x 10in) tin

Ingredients

250g (9oz) butter, diced, plus extra for greasing
125g (4½oz) raspberries, fresh or frozen
1 tbsp golden syrup or honey
1 tsp bicarbonate of soda

1 tsp baking powder
250g (9oz) porridge oats
200g (7oz) plain flour
100g (3½oz) desiccated coconut
100g (3½oz) brown sugar

1 Preheat the oven to 180°C (350°F/Gas Mark 4). Grease the tin with butter and line with baking parchment.

2 Crush the raspberries in a small bowl. If using frozen raspberries, thaw and then break them up with a fork. Place the butter and syrup or honey in a small pan, and melt together slowly until runny. Sprinkle over the bicarbonate of soda and stir the mixture until it is frothy.

3 Place all the remaining ingredients in a large bowl and make a well in the centre. Pour the melted butter mixture into the centre and mix well.

4 Spread half of the mixture into the tin, spread the raspberries over the top, and then cover with the remaining mixture.

5 Place in the oven and bake for 25 minutes until golden. Allow the flapjacks to cool before turning them out and cutting them into rectangles.

Biscotti

These crisp Italian biscuits also make great presents, as they can be prettily packaged and will keep for days.

•makes 25–30

• prep 10 mins
• cook 40–45 mins

❄

• up to 8 weeks

Ingredients

50g (1¾oz) unsalted butter
100g (3½oz) whole almonds, shelled and skinned
225g (8oz) self-raising flour, plus extra for dusting

100g (3½oz) caster sugar
2 eggs
1 tsp vanilla extract

1 Melt the butter in a small pan over a low heat and set aside to cool. Preheat the oven to 180°C (350°F/Gas 4). Line a baking tray with parchment. Spread the almonds out on a non-stick baking tray, and bake in the centre of the oven for 5–10 minutes until slightly coloured, tossing halfway. Allow the almonds to cool until they are comfortable to handle, then roughly chop them.

2 Sift the flour through a fine sieve held over a large bowl. Add the sugar and chopped almonds to the bowl, and stir until well combined.

3 In a separate bowl, whisk together the eggs, vanilla extract, and the melted butter. Gradually pour the egg mixture into the flour, while stirring with a fork. Using your hands, bring the ingredients together to form a dough. If the mixture seems too wet to shape easily, work in a little flour until it is pliable. Turn the dough out onto a lightly floured work surface.

4 With your hands, form the dough into 2 log shapes, each about 20cm (8in) long. Place on the baking tray and bake for 20 minutes in the centre of the oven. Remove the logs from the oven. Cool slightly, then transfer to a chopping board.

5 With a serrated knife, cut the logs on a slant into 3–5cm (1½–2in) thick slices. Put the biscotti on a baking tray and return to the oven for 10 minutes to dry even more. Turn the biscotti with a palette knife, and return to the oven for another 5 minutes. Cool the biscotti on a wire rack to harden them and allow any moisture to escape.

Chocolate brittle

A tower of chocolate brittle makes an impressive end to a good meal. For the best-tasting brittle, buy milk and dark chocolate with a high cocoa content.

- makes 20–30 pieces

- prep 30 mins, plus setting

- up to 12 weeks

Ingredients

For the white chocolate brittle
300g (10oz) white chocolate
150g (5½oz) macadamia nuts

For the milk chocolate brittle
300g (10oz) milk chocolate
100g (3½oz) hazelnuts
100g (3½oz) raisins

For the dark chocolate brittle
300g (10oz) plain chocolate
100g (3½oz) pecans
100g (3½oz) dried cranberries

1 Make each type of chocolate brittle separately. Break the chocolate slabs into small pieces and place them in a small bowl.

2 Melt the chocolate gently in a bowl over a pan of barely simmering water, making sure the bowl does not touch the water. Stir gently with a spoon every so often to make sure all the chocolate pieces melt.

3 Lift the bowl of melted chocolate from the saucepan of water and mix in the dry ingredients. Line a baking tray with some parchment or cling film.

4 Pour the mix into the tray. Allow to cool. Refrigerate until solid. Just before serving, turn out onto a board, remove the parchment, and break into chunks with the tip of a knife.

Chocolate biscuit cake

You can vary the fruit and nuts in this cake to your taste – a handful of chopped cherries and hazelnuts works well too.

• serves 6

• prep 10 mins, plus setting

• 18cm (7in) deep square tin

• up to 8 weeks

Ingredients

150g (5½oz) butter
250g (9oz) dark chocolate, broken into pieces
2 tbsp golden syrup

450g (1lb) digestive biscuits, crushed
handful of plump golden raisins
handful of unskinned almonds, roughly chopped

1 Lightly grease the tin. In a small pan, melt the butter, chocolate, and syrup, then remove from the heat and stir in the biscuits, raisins, and almonds. Mix well, then press the mixture into the tin with the back of a spoon.

2 Transfer to the refrigerator to set completely. Serve sliced into rectangles.

Pistachio and orange biscotti

These fragrant biscotti are delicious served either with coffee or dipped in a glass of sweet dessert wine.

• makes 25–30

• prep 15 mins
• cook 40–45 mins

• up to 8 weeks

Ingredients

100g (3½oz) whole pistachios, shelled
225g (8oz) self-raising flour, plus
   extra for dusting
100g (3½oz) caster sugar
finely grated zest of 1 orange

2 eggs
1 tsp vanilla extract
50g (1¾oz) unsalted butter,
   melted and cooled

1 Preheat the oven to 180°C (350°F/Gas 4). Spread the pistachios on an unlined baking tray. Bake for 5–10 minutes. Allow to cool, rub with a dry, clean tea towel to remove excess skin, then roughly chop them.

2 In a bowl, mix the flour, sugar, zest, and nuts. In a separate bowl, whisk together the eggs, vanilla extract, and butter. Mix the wet and dry ingredients to form a dough.

3 Turn the dough out onto a floured surface and form into 2 logs, each 20 x 7.5cm (8 x 3in). Place them on a baking tray lined with silicone paper and bake for 20 minutes in the centre of the oven. Cool slightly, then cut diagonally into 3–5cm (1¼–2in) thick slices with a serrated knife.

4 Bake for another 15 minutes, turning after 10 minutes, until golden and hard to the touch.

Patisserie and Tarts

Mince pies

The mincemeat in this recipe is quick to prepare and needs no time to mature, making these an easy festive treat to bake.

• makes 18

• prep 20 mins
• cook 10–12 mins

• 7.5cm (3in) round
  pastry cutter
• 6cm (2½in) round
  or shaped cutter
• fairy cake tin

• up to 8 weeks

Ingredients

1 small cooking apple
30g (1oz) butter, melted
85g (3oz) sultanas
85g (3oz) raisins
55g (1¾oz) currants
45g (1½oz) mixed peel, chopped
45g (1½oz) chopped almonds or hazelnuts
finely grated zest of 1 lemon

1 tsp mixed spice
1 tbsp brandy or whisky
30g (1oz) dark brown muscovado sugar
1 small banana, finely diced
500g (1lb 2oz) shortcrust pastry,
   shop-bought
plain flour, for dusting
icing sugar, for dusting

1 Preheat the oven to 190°C (375°F/Gas 5). To make the mincemeat, grate the apple (including the skin) into a large bowl. Add the melted butter, sultanas, raisins, currants, mixed peel, nuts, lemon zest, mixed spice, brandy or whisky, and sugar. Mix until well combined. Add the banana and mix again.

2 Roll out the pastry on a lightly floured work surface to a thickness of 2mm (scant ⅛in) and cut out 18 circles using the larger biscuit cutter. Re-roll the pastry, and cut 18 smaller circles or festive shapes, such as stars.

3 Line fairy cake tins with the larger pastry circles, and place a heaped teaspoon of mincemeat in each case. Top with the smaller circles or shapes.

4 Chill for 10 minutes, then bake for 10–12 minutes or until the pastry is golden. Carefully remove from the tins and cool on a wire rack. Dust with icing sugar to serve.

Store
The pies will keep for 3 days in an airtight container.

Prepare ahead
The pastry can be made 2 days ahead and kept in the refrigerator, wrapped in cling film.

Cinnamon palmiers

Grating frozen butter is a great shortcut when making puff pastry – or use ready-made pastry if pressed for time.

• makes 24

• prep 45 mins,
  plus chilling
• cook 25–30 mins

• up to 8 weeks

Ingredients

250g (9oz) unsalted butter,
  frozen for 30 minutes
250g (9oz) plain flour, plus
  extra for dusting
1 tsp salt
1 egg, lightly beaten, for glazing

For the filling

100g (3½oz) unsalted butter,
  at room temperature
100g (3½oz) soft light brown sugar
4–5 tsp cinnamon, to taste

1 Coarsely grate the butter into a bowl. Sift over the flour and salt. Rub together until crumbly. Pour in 90–100ml (3–3½fl oz) water. Use a fork, then your hands to form a rough dough. Place the dough into a plastic bag and chill in the refrigerator for 20 minutes.

2 On a floured surface, thinly roll the dough into a long rectangle, with short sides 25cm (10in). Take one-third of the pastry and fold into the middle. Fold over the remaining third. Turn it over so the joins are easily sealed when it is re-rolled. Give it a quarter turn. Roll out again to a similar size as the original rectangle. Keep the short sides even in size. Repeat the folding, turning, and rolling. Put the dough back in the bag and chill for 20 minutes. Roll, fold, and turn the pastry twice more, then chill for a final 20 minutes.

3 Meanwhile, for the filling, beat together the butter, sugar, and cinnamon. Preheat the oven to 200°C (400°F/Gas 6). Line 2 baking trays with parchment.

4 Roll the dough out once again. Trim the edges. Spread the filling thinly over the surface. Loosely roll one of the long sides into the middle, and repeat with the other side. Brush with egg wash, press together, then turn over and chill for 10 minutes.

5 Carefully cut into 2cm (¾in) pieces and turn the palmiers face up. Squeeze them to form an oval, and press down lightly with your palm to flatten slightly. Brush the palmiers with the beaten egg and bake for 25–30 minutes. They are ready when golden brown, puffed up, and crisp in the centre. Remove to a wire rack to cool.

Raspberry tartlets with crème pâtissière

For a simple yet tasty alternative to a shortcrust pastry case, try making these biscuit-based crusts instead. Make a few extra and freeze the rest for an instant dessert another time.

Ingredients

For the biscuit case
200g (7oz) digestive or Breton biscuits
50g (1¾oz) caster sugar
100g (3½oz) butter, melted
    and cooled

For the filling
100g (3½oz) caster sugar
40g (1½oz) cornflour
2 eggs
1 tsp vanilla extract
400ml (14fl oz) whole milk
raspberries
icing sugar, for dusting

• makes 6

• prep 20 mins,
plus cooling
• cook 10 mins

• 6 x 10cm (4in)
loose-bottomed
tartlet tins

• tart cases up to
2 months

1 Preheat the oven to 180°C (350°F/Gas 4). To make the base, crush the biscuits in a food processor, or by hand using a rolling pin, until they resemble fine breadcrumbs. Mix the biscuit crumbs, sugar, and melted butter, until the mixture resembles wet sand.

2 Divide the biscuit mixture between the tartlet tins and press it firmly into the bottom of each tin, allowing it to come up the sides as it spreads out. Bake for 10 minutes then set aside to cool. Once cooled, store the tart cases in the refrigerator until needed.

3 For the crème pâtissière, beat together the sugar, cornflour, eggs, and vanilla extract in a bowl. In a saucepan, bring the milk to the boil, and remove from the heat just as it starts to bubble up. Pour the hot milk onto the egg mixture, whisking constantly. Return the custard to the pan, and bring to the boil, whisking constantly to prevent lumps. As the custard heats it will thicken considerably. At this point reduce the heat to low and cook for a further 2–3 minutes.

4 Turn the thickened crème pâtissière out into a bowl, cover the surface of it with cling film (to prevent a skin forming), and set it aside to cool. Once it is cold, beat it well with a wooden spoon before use.

5 When you are ready to assemble the tartlets, spoon or pipe the crème patisserie into the cases. Top with raspberries, and dust with icing sugar to serve. The tart cases can be chilled for up to 3 days, and the crème patisserie for up to 2 days, well covered.

Danish pastries

Although these deliciously buttery pastries take a little time to prepare, the home-baked taste is incomparable.

• makes 18

• prep 30 mins,
plus chilling
and rising
• cook 15–20 mins

❄

• up to 4 weeks

Ingredients

150ml (5fl oz) warm milk
2 tsp dried yeast
30g (1oz) caster sugar
2 eggs, plus 1 egg, beaten, for glazing
475g (1lb 1oz) strong white bread flour,
   sifted, plus extra for dusting
½ tsp salt
vegetable oil, for greasing
250g (9oz) chilled butter

For the filling

200g (7oz) good-quality cherry,
   strawberry, or apricot jam,
   or compote

1 Mix the milk, yeast, and 1 tablespoon sugar. Cover for 20 minutes, then beat in the eggs. Place the flour, salt, and remaining sugar in a bowl. Make a well and pour in the yeast mix. Mix the ingredients into a soft dough. Knead for 15 minutes on a floured surface until soft. Place the dough in a lightly oiled bowl, cover with cling film and refrigerate for 15 minutes.

2 On a lightly floured surface, roll out the dough to a square, about 25 x 25cm (10 x 10in). Cut the butter into 3–4 slices, each about 12 x 6 x 1cm (5 x 2½ x ½in). Lay the butter slices on one-half of the dough, leaving a border of 1–2cm (½–¾in). Fold the other half of the dough over the top, pressing the edges with a rolling pin to seal.

3 Generously flour and roll the dough out into a rectangle 3 times as long as it is wide, and 1cm (½in) thick. Fold the top third down into the middle, then the bottom third back over it. Wrap and chill for 15 minutes. Repeat the rolling and folding of the dough twice more, chilling for 15 minutes each time.

4 Roll onto a floured surface to 5mm–1cm (¼–½in) thick. Cut into 10 x 10cm (4 x 4in) squares. With a sharp knife, make diagonal cuts from each corner to within 1cm (½in) of the centre.

5 Put 1 teaspoon of jam in the centre of each square and fold each corner into the centre. Spoon more jam on the centre, transfer to a lined baking tray, and cover with a dry, clean tea towel. Leave in a warm place for 30 minutes until risen. Preheat the oven to 200°C (400°F/ Gas 6). Brush with egg wash and bake at the top of the oven for 15–20 minutes until golden. Leave to cool slightly then transfer to a wire rack.

Chocolate éclairs

Close cousins of the popular profiterole, these can be easily adapted: try a chocolate orange topping and an orange cream or crème pâtissière filling.

• makes 30

• prep 30 mins
• cook 25–30 mins

• piping bag
and 1cm (½in) plain
nozzle

• up to 12 weeks,
unfilled

Ingredients

75g (2½oz) unsalted butter
125g (4½oz) plain flour, sifted
3 eggs

500ml (16fl oz) double cream
150g (5½oz) good-quality dark chocolate,
  broken into pieces

1 Preheat the oven to 200°C (400°F/Gas 6). Melt the butter in a pan with 200ml (7fl oz) cold water, then bring to the boil, remove from the heat, and stir in the flour. Beat with a wooden spoon until well combined.

2 Lightly beat the eggs and add to the flour and butter mixture, a little at a time, whisking constantly. Continue whisking until the mixture is smooth and glossy, and comes away easily from the sides of the pan. Transfer to the piping bag.

3 Pipe 10cm (4in) lengths of the mixture onto 2 baking trays lined with parchment, cutting the end of the length of pastry from the bag with a wet knife. You should have around 30 in all. Bake for 20–25 minutes or until golden brown, then remove from the oven and make a slit down the side of each. Return to the oven for 5 minutes for the insides to cook through. Then remove and leave to cool.

4 Place the cream in a mixing bowl and beat with an electric whisk until soft peaks form. Spoon or pipe into each éclair. Place the chocolate pieces in a heatproof bowl. Sit the bowl over a pan of simmering water, making sure the bowl does not touch the water, and leave the chocolate to melt. Spoon over the éclairs and leave to dry before serving.

Raspberry macarons

The skill in making perfect macarons lies in the technique – gentle folding and piping the mix vertically downwards should help.

• makes 20

• prep 30 mins
• cook 18–20 mins

• piping bag and small, plain nozzle

Ingredients

100g (3½oz) icing sugar
75g (2½oz) ground almonds
2 large egg whites, at room temperature
75g (2½oz) granulated sugar
3–4 drops of pink food colouring

For the filling
150g (5½oz) mascarpone
50g (1¾oz) seedless raspberry conserve

1 Preheat the oven to 150°C (300°F/Gas 2). Line 2 baking trays with silicone paper. Draw on 3cm (1¼in) circles with a pencil, leaving 3cm (1¼in) gap between each. In a food processor, whizz together the icing sugar and almonds until very finely mixed and smooth.

2 In a bowl, whisk the egg whites until they form stiff peaks. Add the granulated sugar, a little at a time, whisking well between each addition. Whisk in the food colouring.

3 Fold in the almond mixture, a spoonful at a time, until just mixed. Transfer the mix to the piping bag. Holding the bag vertically, pipe meringue into the centre of each circle.

4 Bake in the centre of the oven for 18–20 minutes until the surface is firm. Leave to cool on the trays for 15–20 minutes, before transferring to a wire rack to cool.

5 For the filling, beat the mascarpone and raspberry conserve until smooth and transfer to the (cleaned) piping bag used earlier, with the same nozzle. Pipe a blob of the filling onto the flat side of half the macarons and sandwich together with the rest of the halves. Serve the same day, or the macarons will go soft.

Chocolate truffles

Indulgent chocolate balls, so addictive, they should be kept under lock and key. You can also roll them in chopped, toasted almonds or grated white chocolate.

• makes 12–14

• prep 15 mins,
plus cooling
and setting

Ingredients

125g (4½oz) good-quality dark chocolate, plus 25g (scant 1oz) good-quality dark chocolate, finely grated
drizzle of Baileys Irish Cream or brandy

25g (scant 1oz) Brazil nuts, finely chopped
50g (1¾oz) dried cherries, chopped

1 Break the whole chocolate into pieces and place them in a heatproof bowl. Sit the bowl over a pan of simmering water, making sure the bowl does not touch the water. Stir the chocolate until smooth, then stir in the Baileys or brandy and add the nuts and cherries.

2 Leave to cool for 30 minutes, then scoop up a generous teaspoonful and form into a ball. Roll in the grated chocolate so the ball is covered evenly, then place on baking parchment for 30 minutes or until set. Repeat with the rest of the chocolate mixture. Serve as a sweet treat with coffee.

Banana and Nutella crumble tartlets

These unusual little tartlets have to be tasted to be believed and will be a hit with adults and children alike. Serve warm or at room temperature with cream and eat on the day they are made.

Ingredients

For the pastry
175g (6oz) plain flour, plus
  extra for dusting
25g (scant 1oz) caster sugar
100g (3½oz) unsalted butter, softened
1 egg yolk, beaten with 2 tbsp cold water

For the filling
25g (scant 1oz) plain flour
25g (scant 1oz) soft light brown sugar
10g (¼oz) desiccated coconut
25g (scant 1oz) butter, softened
2–3 bananas, not too ripe
4 tbsp Nutella

• makes 6

• prep 20 mins,
  plus chilling
• cook 35 mins

• 6 x 10cm (4in)
loose-bottomed
fluted tart tins,
• baking beans

• pastry cases up
  to 2 months

1 To make the pastry, rub the flour, caster sugar, and butter together, by hand or in a food processor, until they resemble fine breadcrumbs. Add the egg yolk and bring the mixture together to form a soft dough; add a little water if needed. Wrap and chill for 30 minutes.

2 Preheat the oven to 180°C (350°F/Gas 4). Roll out the pastry on a floured surface to 3mm (⅛in) thick and use to line the tart tins, leaving an overlapping edge of 1cm (½in). Trim off any excess pastry that hangs down further than this. Prick the bottom with a fork, line with greaseproof paper, and fill with baking beans. Place on a baking tray and bake for 15 minutes. Remove the beans and paper and return to the oven for a further 5 minutes if the centres look uncooked. Trim off any ragged edges from the cases while still warm. Increase the temperature to 200°C (400°F/Gas 6).

3 For the filling, mix together the flour, soft light brown sugar, and coconut in a large bowl. Rub in the butter by hand, making sure that the mixture isn't too well mixed, and that there are some larger lumps of butter remaining.

4 Peel and slice the bananas into 1cm (½in) slices across on a diagonal slant, and use pieces to create a single layer on the bottom of the tart cases, breaking them to fit if needed. Spread 1 tablespoon Nutella over the banana to cover. Divide the crumble mix between the tarts and loosely spread it over, taking care not to pack it down. Bake for 15 minutes until the crumble has started to brown.

Chocolate palmiers

Once the pastry is prepared, palmiers are quick and tasty snacks that are portable enough to take on a picnic.

• makes 24

• prep 45 mins, plus chilling
• cook 25–30 mins

• up to 8 weeks

Ingredients

250g (9oz) unsalted butter, frozen for 30 minutes
250g (9oz) plain flour, plus extra for dusting
1 tsp salt
1 egg, lightly beaten, for glazing

For the filling
150g (5½oz) dark chocolate, broken into pieces

1 Coarsely grate the butter into a bowl. Sift over the flour and salt. Rub together until crumbly. Pour in 90–100ml (3–3½fl oz) water. Use a fork, then your hands to form a rough dough. Place the dough into a plastic bag and chill in the refrigerator for 20 minutes.

2 On a floured surface, thinly roll the dough into a long rectangle, with short sides 25cm (10in). Take one-third of the pastry and fold into the middle. Fold over the remaining third. Turn it over so the joins are easily sealed when it is re-rolled. Give it a quarter turn. Roll out again to a similar size as the original rectangle. Keep the short sides even in size. Repeat the folding, turning, and rolling. Put the dough back in the bag and chill for 20 minutes. Roll, fold, and turn the pastry twice more, then chill for a final 20 minutes.

3 Meanwhile, for the filling, melt the chocolate in a bowl set over a pan of simmering water, making sure the bowl does not touch the water. Set aside to cool. Preheat the oven to 200°C (400°F/Gas 6). Line 2 baking trays with parchment.

4 Roll the dough to a rectangle 5mm (¼in) thick. Spread the filling over. Roll up one of the long sides of the pastry nearly into the middle, and repeat with the other side. Brush the sides with egg and roll them together. Turn over and chill for 10 minutes.

5 Trim the ends of the roll and cut it into 2cm (¾in) pieces. Turn the pastries face up, press them together to form an oval shape, and press down to bring the roll together.

6 Transfer to the baking trays, brush with a little beaten egg, and bake at the top of the oven for 25–30 minutes. They are ready when golden brown, puffed up, and crisp in the centre. Remove to a wire rack to cool.

Jam doughnuts

Doughnuts are surprisingly easy to make. These are light, airy, and taste far nicer than any shop-bought varieties.

• makes 12

• prep 30 mins,
  plus rising
  and proving
• cook 5–10 mins

• oil thermometer
• piping bag and
  thin nozzle

Ingredients

150ml (5fl oz) milk
75g (2½oz) unsalted butter
½ tsp vanilla extract
2 tsp dried yeast
75g (2½oz) caster sugar
2 eggs, beaten
425g (15oz) plain flour, preferably
   "00" grade, plus extra for dusting
½ tsp salt
1 litre (1¾pints) sunflower oil, for
   deep-frying, plus extra for greasing

For coating and filling
caster sugar, for coating
250g (9oz) good-quality jam
   (raspberry, strawberry, or cherry),
   processed until smooth

1 Heat the milk, butter, and vanilla extract in a pan until the butter melts. Cool until tepid. Whisk in the yeast and a tablespoon of sugar. Cover and leave for 10 minutes. Mix in the eggs.

2 Sift the flour and salt into a large bowl. Stir in the remaining sugar. Make a well in the flour and add the milk mixture. Bring together to form a rough dough. Turn the dough out onto a floured surface and knead for 10 minutes until soft and pliable. Put in an oiled bowl and cover with cling film. Keep it warm for 2 hours until doubled in size.

3 On a floured surface, knock back the dough and divide into 12 equal pieces. Roll them between your palms to form balls. Place on baking trays, spaced well apart. Cover with cling film and a dry, clean tea towel. Leave in a warm place for 1–2 hours until doubled in size.

4 In a large, heavy-based saucepan heat the oil to 170–180°C (340–350°F) at a depth of 10cm (4in), keeping the lid nearby for safety. Slide the doughnuts off the trays. Do not worry if they are flatter on one side. Carefully lower the doughnuts, 3 at a time, into the hot oil, rounded side down. Turn after about 1 minute. Remove with a slotted spoon when golden brown all over. Switch off the heat. Drain on kitchen paper, then, while still hot, toss them in caster sugar. Cool before filling.

5 Put the jam into the piping bag. Pierce each doughnut on the side and insert the nozzle. Gently squirt in about a tablespoon of jam until it almost starts to spill out. Dust the hole with a little more sugar and serve.

Strawberries and cream macarons

The art of macaron making can be a little tricky to master, but the end result is well worth the effort.

Ingredients

100g (3½oz) icing sugar
75g (2½oz) ground almonds
2 large egg whites,
   at room temperature
75g (2½oz) granulated sugar

For the filling
200ml (7fl oz) double cream
5–10 very large strawberries, preferably
   the same diameter as the macarons

• makes 20

• prep 30 mins
• cook 18–20 mins

• piping bag and
small, plain nozzle

1 Preheat the oven to 150°C (300°F/Gas 2). Line 2 baking trays with silicone paper. Trace twenty 3cm (1¼in) circles, leaving 3cm (1¼in) between circles. Invert the paper.

2 In a food processor, whizz together the icing sugar and almonds to a very fine meal. In a large bowl, whisk the egg whites to stiff peaks using an electric whisk. Whilst whisking, add the the granulated sugar, a little at a time, whisking well between additions. The meringue mixture should be very stiff at this point. Gently fold in the almond mixture, a spoonful at a time, until just incorporated.

3 Transfer the macaron mix to the piping bag, placing the bag into a bowl to help. Using the guidelines, pipe the mix into the centre of each circle, holding the bag vertically. Try to keep the disks even in size and volume; the mix will spread only very slightly.

4 Bang the baking trays down a few times if there are any peaks left in the centre. Bake in the centre of the oven for 18–20 minutes until the surface is set firm. Test one shell: a firm prod with a finger should crack the top of the macaron. Leave for 15–20 minutes, then transfer to a wire rack to cool completely.

5 For the filling, whisk the cream until thick; a soft whip would ooze out the sides and soften the shells. Transfer the cream into the (cleaned) piping bag used earlier, with the same nozzle. Pipe a blob of the whipped cream onto the flat side of half the macarons. Slice the strawberries widthways into thin slices, the same diameter as the macarons. Place a slice of strawberry on top of the cream filling of each macaron. Add the remaining macaron shells and sandwich gently. The filling should peek out. Serve the same day, or the macarons will go soft.

Coconut cream tartlets

Rich, buttery shortcrust tartlets can be baked in bulk and frozen for future use. Just crisp them up in a hot oven for a few minutes before filling, here with a deliciously thick coconut cream.

• makes 4

• prep 30 mins, plus chilling
• cook 20 mins

• 4 x 12cm (5in) loose-bottomed fluted tart tins

Ingredients

For the pastry
150g (5½oz) plain flour, plus extra for dusting
100g (3½oz) unsalted butter, diced, plus extra for greasing
50g (1¾oz) caster sugar
1 egg yolk
½ tsp vanilla extract

For the filling
400ml tin coconut milk
240ml (8½fl oz) whole milk
4 egg yolks
50g (1¾oz) caster sugar
4 tbsp cornflour
1 tsp vanilla extract
4 tbsp desiccated coconut

1 Preheat the oven to 200°C (400°F/Gas 6). Lightly grease the tart tins. To make the pastry, rub the flour and butter together in a bowl with your fingertips until the mixture resembles fine breadcrumbs. Stir in the sugar. Add the egg yolk and vanilla to the flour mixture and bring together to form a smooth dough, adding 1–2 tablespoons cold water if needed. Wrap in cling film and chill for 30 minutes.

2 For the filling, heat the coconut milk and whole milk in a small non-stick saucepan, until just boiling. Whisk the egg yolks, sugar, cornflour, and vanilla together in a heatproof medium bowl or large jug. Gradually pour in the hot milk mixture, whisking constantly. Pour the coconut custard back into the pan and stir, with a wooden spoon, over a medium heat, until it thickens. Remove the pan, cover the coconut custard with greaseproof paper, and set aside to cool.

3 Divide the pastry equally into 4 parts. Roll out one-quarter of the dough on a well-floured surface to a circle large enough to line one of the tins. Place the pastry in the tin and trim the edges. Prick the bottom with a fork and place on a baking tray. Repeat using the remaining pastry. Chill for 30 minutes.

4 Line each tartlet case with foil, pressing it down well. Bake for 5 minutes, then remove the foil, and bake for a further 5 minutes. Set aside to cool.

5 In a small, dry frying pan, lightly toast the coconut over a medium heat, shaking the pan occasionally. Remove the pastry cases from the tins. An hour before serving, spoon the cooled coconut custard into the pastry cases and chill for 1 hour. Sprinkle with the toasted coconut to serve.

Baklava

This crispy Middle Eastern confection, filled with chopped nuts and spices and drenched in honey syrup, has long been a favourite.

Ingredients

250g (9oz) shelled unsalted pistachio nuts, coarsely chopped
250g (9oz) walnut pieces, coarsely chopped
250g (9oz) caster sugar
2 tsp ground cinnamon
large pinch of ground cloves

500g pack of filo pastry
250g (9oz) unsalted butter, plus extra for greasing
250ml (9fl oz) honey
juice of 1 lemon
3 tbsp orange flower water

1 Set aside 3–4 tablespoons of the chopped pistachios for decoration. Place the remainder in a bowl with the walnuts, 50g (1¾oz) of the sugar, cinnamon, and cloves. Stir to mix.

2 Preheat the oven to 180°C (350°F/Gas 4). Lay a damp, clean tea towel on a work surface, unroll the filo sheets on it, and cover with a second dampened towel. Melt the butter in a small saucepan. Brush the baking tin with a little butter and line with a sheet of filo.

3 Brush the filo with butter, and gently press it into the corners and sides of the tin. Lay another sheet on top, brush it with butter, and press it into the tin as before. Continue layering the filo, buttering each sheet, until one-third has been used. Scatter half the nut filling over the top sheet. Layer the remaining sheets in the same manner. Trim off the excess with a knife. Brush with butter, and pour any remaining butter on top.

4 With a small knife, cut diagonal lines, 1cm (½in) deep, in the filo to mark out 4cm (1½in) diamond shapes. Do not press down when cutting. Bake on the low shelf of the oven for 1¼–1½ hours until golden and a skewer inserted in the centre comes out clean.

5 For the syrup, place the remaining sugar and 250ml (9fl oz) water in a pan, and heat until dissolved, stirring occasionally. Pour in the honey and stir to mix. Boil for about 25 minutes, without stirring, until the syrup reaches the soft ball stage, 115°C (239°F) on the sugar thermometer. To test without a thermometer, take the pan off the heat and dip a teaspoon in the syrup. Let the syrup cool for 2–3 seconds, then take a little between your fingers; a soft ball should form. Remove the syrup from the heat and let it cool to lukewarm. Add the lemon juice and orange flower water. Remove the tin from the oven and immediately pour the syrup over the pastries.

6 With a sharp knife, cut along the marked lines, then let the pastries cool. Cut through the marked lines completely. Carefully lift out the pastries with a palette knife and sprinkle the top of each pastry with the reserved chopped pistachio nuts.

Apricot pastries

Prepare the pastry the night before, so that 30 minutes of rising in the morning and a quick bake will give you fresh pastries in time for coffee.

• makes 18

• prep 30 mins, plus chilling and rising
• cook 15–20 mins

❄

• up to 4 weeks

Ingredients

150ml (5fl oz) warm milk
2 tsp dried yeast
30g (1oz) caster sugar
2 eggs, plus 1 egg, beaten, for glazing
475g (1lb 1oz) strong white bread flour, sifted, plus extra for dusting
½ tsp salt

vegetable oil, for greasing
250g (9oz) chilled butter

For the filling
200g (7oz) apricot jam
2 x 400g cans apricot halves

1 Mix the milk, yeast, and 1 tablespoon sugar. Cover for 20 minutes, then beat in the eggs. Place the flour, salt, and remaining sugar in a bowl. Make a well and pour in the yeast mix. Mix the ingredients into a soft dough. Knead for 15 minutes on a floured surface until soft. Place the dough in a lightly oiled bowl, cover with cling film and refrigerate for 15 minutes.

2 On a lightly floured surface, roll out the dough to a square, about 25 x 25cm (10 x 10in). Cut the butter into 3–4 slices, each about 12 x 6 x 1cm (5 x 2½ x ½in). Lay the butter slices on one-half of the dough, leaving a border of 1–2cm (½–¾in). Fold the other half of the dough over the top, pressing the edges with a rolling pin to seal.

3 Generously flour and roll the dough out into a rectangle 3 times as long as it is wide, and 1cm (½in) thick. Fold the top third down into the middle, then the bottom third back over it. Wrap and chill for 15 minutes. Repeat the rolling and folding action twice more, chilling for 15 minutes each time. Roll half the dough out on a well-floured work surface to a 30cm (12in) square. Trim the edges and cut out nine 10cm (4in) squares. Repeat with the remaining dough.

4 If needed, purée the apricot jam until smooth. Spread 1 tablespoon of jam over a square, leaving a border of about 1cm (½in). Take 2 apricot halves and trim a little off their bottoms if too chunky. Place an apricot half in 2 opposite corners of the square. Take the 2 corners without apricots and fold them into the middle. They should only partially cover the apricot halves. Repeat to fill all the pastries. Place on lined baking trays, cover, and leave to rise in a warm place for 30 minutes until puffed up.

5 Preheat the oven to 200°C (400°F/Gas 6). Brush the pastries with beaten egg and bake in the top third of the oven for 15–20 minutes until golden. Melt the remaining jam and brush over the pastries to glaze. Cool for 5 minutes, then transfer to a wire rack.

Churros

These cinnamon- and sugar-sprinkled snacks from Spain take minutes to make and will be devoured just as quickly. Try them dipped in hot chocolate.

• serves 2–4

• prep 10 mins
• cook 5–10 mins

• oil thermometer
• piping bag and
2cm (¾in) nozzle

Ingredients

25g (scant 1oz) unsalted butter
200g (7oz) plain flour
50g (1¾oz) caster sugar
1 tsp baking powder

1 litre (1¾ pints) sunflower oil,
   for deep-frying
1 tsp cinnamon

1 Measure 200ml (7fl oz) boiling water into a jug. Add the butter and stir until it melts. Sift together the flour, half the sugar, and the baking powder into a bowl. Make a well in the centre and slowly pour in the hot butter liquid, beating continuously, until you have a thick paste; you may not need all the liquid. Leave the mixture to cool and rest for 5 minutes.

2 Pour the oil into a large, heavy-based saucepan to a depth of at least 10cm (4in), and heat it to 170–180°C (340–350°F). Keep the correct-sized saucepan lid nearby and never leave the hot oil unattended. Regulate the temperature, making sure it remains even, or the churros will burn.

3 Place the cooled mixture into the piping bag. Pipe 7cm (scant 3in) lengths of the dough into the hot oil, using a pair of scissors to snip off the ends. Do not crowd the pan, or the temperature of the oil will go down. Cook the churros for 1–2 minutes on each side, turning them when they are golden brown. When done, remove the churros from the oil with a slotted spoon and drain on kitchen paper. Switch off the heat.

4 Mix the remaining sugar and the cinnamon together on a plate, and toss the churros in the mixture while still hot. Leave to cool for 5–10 minutes before serving while still warm.

Profiteroles

Cream-filled choux pastry buns drizzled with chocolate sauce make for a delightfully decadent dessert.

• makes 4

• prep 20 mins, plus cooling
• cook 22 mins

• 2 x piping bags with 1cm (½in) plain nozzle and 5mm (¼in) star nozzle

• up to 12 weeks, unfilled

Ingredients

60g (2oz) plain flour
50g (1¾oz) unsalted butter
2 eggs, lightly beaten

For the filling and topping

400ml (14fl oz) double cream
200g (7oz) good-quality dark chocolate, broken into pieces
25g (scant 1oz) butter
2 tbsp golden syrup

1 Preheat the oven to 220°C (425°F/Gas 7). Line 2 large baking trays with parchment. Sift the flour into a large bowl, holding the sieve high to aerate the flour.

2 Place the butter and 150ml (5fl oz) water into a small saucepan, and heat gently until melted. Bring to the boil, remove from the heat, and tip in the flour all at once. Beat with a wooden spoon until smooth; the mixture should form a ball. Cool for 10 minutes. Gradually add the eggs, beating very well after each addition to incorporate. Continue adding the eggs, little by little, to form a stiff, smooth, and shiny paste.

3 Spoon the mixture into the piping bag fitted with the plain nozzle. Pipe walnut-sized rounds, set well apart. Bake for 20 minutes until risen and golden. Remove from the oven and slit the side of each bun to allow the steam to escape. Return to the oven for 2 minutes to crisp, then transfer to a wire rack to cool completely.

4 Before serving, pour 100ml (3½fl oz) cream into a pan and whip the rest until just peaking. Add the chocolate, butter, and syrup to the cream in the pan, and heat gently until melted. Pile the whipped cream into the piping bag fitted with the star nozzle. Open the buns and fill them with the cream. Arrange the buns on a serving plate or cake stand. Stir the sauce, pour over the buns and serve immediately.

Cannoli

Originally from Sicily, these crisp pastries are filled with glacé fruits and ricotta cheese. Their name translates to mean "little tubes".

• makes 16

• prep 30 mins, plus cooling
• cook 20 mins

• oil thermometer
• cannoli moulds
• piping bag and nozzle (optional)

• up to 12 weeks, unbaked

Ingredients

175g (6oz) plain flour, plus extra for dusting
pinch of salt
60g (2oz) butter
45g (1½oz) caster sugar
1 egg, beaten
2–3 tbsp dry white wine or Marsala
1 egg white, lightly beaten
1 litre (1¾ pints) sunflower oil,
    for deep-frying

For the filling

60g (2oz) dark chocolate, grated
    or very finely chopped
350g (12oz) ricotta cheese
60g (2oz) icing sugar, plus extra
    for dusting
finely grated zest of 1 orange
60g (2oz) chopped glacé fruits
    or candied citrus peel

1 For the pastry, sift the flour and salt into a bowl, and rub in the butter. Stir in the sugar and mix in the egg and enough wine to make a soft dough. Knead until smooth.

2 Roll out the pastry thinly and cut into 16 squares, each measuring roughly 7.5cm (3in). Dust 4 cannoli moulds with flour and wrap a pastry square loosely around each on the diagonal, dampening the edges with the egg white and pressing them together to seal.

3 Pour the oil into a large, heavy-based saucepan to a depth of 10cm (4in), and heat it to 180°C (350°F). Keep the correct-sized saucepan lid nearby and never leave the hot oil unattended. Deep-fry for 3–4 minutes or until the pastry is golden and crisp. Drain on a plate lined with kitchen paper, and when cool enough to handle, carefully twist the metal tubes so you can pull them out of the pastry. Cook 3 more batches in the same way.

4 For the filling, mix together all the ingredients. When the pastry tubes are cold, pipe or spoon the filling into them. Dust with icing sugar to serve.

Tangerine macarons

Sharp, zesty tangerines are used rather than the more usual oranges, to counter-balance the meringues.

Ingredients

100g (3½oz) icing sugar
75g (2½oz) ground almonds
1 scant tsp finely grated tangerine zest
2 large egg whites, at room temperature
75g (2½oz) granulated sugar
3–4 drops orange food colouring

For the filling
100g (3½oz) icing sugar
50g (1¾oz) unsalted butter,
   at room temperature
1 tbsp tangerine juice
1 scant tsp finely grated tangerine zest

1 Preheat the oven to 150°C (300°F/Gas 2). Line 2 baking trays with silicone paper. Draw on 3cm (1¼in) circles with a pencil, leaving 3cm (1¼in) gap between each one. Whizz the icing sugar and ground almonds in a food processor with a blade attachment, until finely mixed. Add the tangerine zest and whizz briefly.

2 In a bowl, whisk the egg whites to form stiff peaks. Add the granulated sugar, a little at a time, whisking well with each addition. Whisk in the food colouring.

3 Fold in the almond mixture, a spoonful at a time. Transfer to the piping bag. Holding the bag vertically, pipe meringue into the centre of each circle.

4 Bake in the middle of the oven for 18–20 minutes until the surface is set firm. Leave the macarons to cool on the baking trays for 15–20 minutes and then transfer to a wire rack to cool completely.

5 For the filling, cream together the icing sugar, butter, tangerine juice, and zest until smooth. Transfer the cream into the (cleaned) piping bag using the same nozzle. Pipe a blob of icing onto the flat side of half the macarons, and sandwich with the rest. Serve the same day, or the macarons will start to go soft.

Monts Blancs

If using sweetened chestnut purée, omit the caster sugar in the filling.

• makes 8

• prep 20 mins
• cook 45–60 mins

• large metal
mixing bowl
• 10cm (4in) pastry
cutter

Ingredients

4 egg whites, at room temperature
about 240g (8¾oz) caster sugar
sunflower oil, for greasing

For the filling
435g can sweetened or unsweetened
   chestnut purée
100g (3½oz) caster sugar (optional)
1 tsp vanilla extract
500ml (16fl oz) double cream
icing sugar, for dusting

1 Preheat the oven to the lowest setting, around 120°C (250°F/Gas ¼). Put the egg whites into a large, clean metal bowl and whisk them until they are stiff, and leave peaks when the whisk is removed from the egg whites. Gradually add the sugar 2 tablespoons at a time, whisking well between each addition, until you have added at least half. Gently fold the remaining sugar into the egg whites, trying to lose as little air as possible.

2 Lightly grease the pastry cutter. Line 2 baking sheets with silicone paper. Place the pastry cutter on the sheets, and spoon the meringue mixture into the ring, to a depth of 3cm (1¼in). Smooth over the top and gently remove the ring. Repeat until there are 4 meringue bases on each baking sheet.

3 Bake the meringues in the centre of the oven for 45 minutes if you like them chewy, otherwise bake for 1 hour. Turn off the oven and leave the meringues to cool inside, to stop them cracking. Remove to a wire rack to cool completely.

4 Put the chestnut purée in a bowl with the caster sugar (if using), vanilla extract, and 4 tablespoons of double cream, and beat together until smooth. Push through a fine sieve to make a light, fluffy filling. In a separate bowl, whisk up the remaining double cream until firm.

5 Gently smooth 1 tablespoon chestnut filling over the top of the meringues, using a palette knife to smooth the surface level. Top each meringue with a spoonful of whipped cream, smoothed round with a palette knife to give the appearance of soft peaks. Dust with icing sugar and serve.

Almond crescents

Butter, sugar, and ground almonds are combined here to make a divine filling for these light and flaky crescent-shaped Danish pastries.

- makes 18

- prep 30 mins,
  plus chilling
  and rising
- cook 15–20 mins

- up to 4 weeks

Ingredients

150ml (5fl oz) warm milk
2 tsp dried yeast
30g (1oz) caster sugar
2 eggs, plus 1 egg, beaten, for glazing
475g (1lb 1oz) strong white bread flour,
   sifted, plus extra for dusting
½ tsp salt
vegetable oil, for greasing

250g (9oz) chilled butter
icing sugar, to serve

For the almond paste
25g (scant 1oz) unsalted butter,
   at room temperature
75g (2½oz) caster sugar
75g (2½oz) ground almonds

1 Mix the milk, yeast, and 1 tablespoon sugar. Cover for 20 minutes, then beat in the eggs. Place the flour, salt, and remaining sugar in a bowl. Make a well and pour in the yeast mix. Mix the ingredients into a soft dough. Knead for 15 minutes on a floured surface until soft. Place the dough in a lightly oiled bowl, cover with cling film and refrigerate for 15 minutes.

2 On a lightly floured surface, roll out the dough to a square, about 25 x 25cm (10 x 10in). Cut the butter into 3–4 slices, each about 12 x 6 x 1cm (5 x 2½ x ½in). Lay the butter slices on one-half of the dough, leaving a border of 1–2cm (½–¾in). Fold the other half of the dough over the top, pressing the edges with a rolling pin to seal. Generously flour and roll the dough out into a rectangle 3 times as long as it is wide, and 1cm (½in) thick. Fold the top third down into the middle, then the bottom third back over it. Wrap and chill for 15 minutes. Repeat the rolling and folding of the dough twice more, chilling for 15 minutes each time.

3 Preheat the oven to 200°C (400°F/Gas 6). Roll half the dough out on a floured surface to a 30cm (12in) square. Trim the edges and cut out nine 10cm (4in) squares. Repeat with the remaining dough.

4 For the almond paste, cream together the butter and caster sugar, then beat in the ground almonds until smooth. Divide the paste into 18 small balls. Roll each one into a sausage shape a little shorter than the length of the dough squares. Place a roll of the paste at one edge of the square, leaving a gap of 2cm (¾in) between it and the edge. Press it down.

5 Brush the clear edge with egg and fold the pastry over the paste, pressing it down. Use a sharp knife to make 4 cuts into the folded edge to within 1–2cm (½–¾in) of the sealed edge. Transfer to baking trays lined with parchment, cover, and leave in a warm place for 30 minutes until puffed up. Bend the edges in. Brush with beaten egg and bake in the top third of the oven for 15–20 minutes, until golden brown. Cool, and dust icing sugar over the pastries before serving.

Cinnamon rolls

If you prefer, leave the rolls to prove overnight in the refrigerator and bake in time for a breakfast treat.

• makes 10–12

• prep 40 mins,
plus rising
and proving
• cook 25–30 mins

• 30cm (12in) round
springform cake tin

❄

• up to 4 weeks

Ingredients

120ml (4fl oz) milk
100g (3½oz) unsalted butter,
    plus extra for greasing
2 tsp dried yeast
50g (1¾oz) caster sugar
550g (1¼lb) plain flour, sifted,
    plus extra for dusting
1 tsp salt
1 egg, plus 2 egg yolks
vegetable oil, for greasing

For the filling and glaze

3 tbsp cinnamon
100g (3½oz) soft light brown sugar
25g (scant 1oz) unsalted butter, melted
1 egg, lightly beaten
4 tbsp caster sugar

1 In a pan, heat 120ml (4fl oz) water, the milk, and butter until just melted. Let it cool. When just warm, whisk in the yeast and a tablespoon of sugar, and cover for 10 minutes. Place the flour, salt, and remaining sugar in a large bowl. Make a well in centre of the dry ingredients and pour in the warm milk mixture.

2 Whisk the egg and egg yolks, and add to the mixture. Combine to form a rough dough. Place on a floured surface and knead for 10 minutes. Add some extra flour if it's too sticky. Place in an oiled bowl, cover with cling film and keep in a warm place for 2 hours until well risen.

3 For the filling, mix 2 tablespoons of cinnamon with the brown sugar. When the dough has risen, turn it onto a floured work surface and gently knock it back. Roll it out into a rectangle about 40 x 30cm (16 x 12in) and brush with melted butter. Scatter with the filling. Leave a 1cm (½in) border on one side and brush it with beaten egg.

4 Press the filling with the palm of your hand to ensure it sticks to the dough. Roll the dough up, working towards the border. Do not roll too tightly. Cut into 10–12 equal pieces with a serrated knife, taking care not to squash the rolls. Grease and line the tin. Pack in the rolls, cover, and prove for 1–2 hours until well risen.

5 Preheat the oven to 180°C (350°F/Gas 4). Brush with egg and bake for 25–30 minutes. For the glaze, heat 3 tablespoons water and 2 tablespoons sugar until dissolved. Brush over the rolls. Sprinkle over a mix of the remaining caster sugar and cinnamon, before turning out onto a wire rack to cool.

Flaky pear tartlets

These are a party favourite, a spectacular contrast of hot and cold, and need very little last-minute preparation.

Ingredients

• serves 8

• prep 35–40 mins,
  plus chilling
• cook 30–40 mins

450g (1lb) ready-made puff pastry
1 egg, beaten with ½ tsp salt, for glazing
4 pears
juice of 1 lemon
50g (1¾oz) sugar

For the caramel sauce
150g (5½oz) caster sugar
125ml (4fl oz) double cream

For the Chantilly cream
125ml (4fl oz) double cream
1–2 tsp icing sugar
½ tsp vanilla essence

1 Sprinkle 2 baking trays with cold water. Roll out the puff pastry dough, cut in half lengthways, then cut diagonally at 10cm (4in) intervals along the length of each piece, to make 8 diamond shapes. Transfer to the trays, and brush with the glaze. With the tip of a knife, score a border around each. Chill for 15 minutes in the refrigerator.

2 Preheat the oven to 220°C (425°F/Gas 7). Bake the cases for about 15 minutes, until they start to brown, then reduce the temperature to 190°C (375°F/Gas 5) and bake for a further 20–25 minutes until golden and crisp. Transfer to wire racks to cool, then cut out the lid from each case, and scoop out any under-cooked pastry from inside.

3 For the caramel sauce, place 120ml (4fl oz) water in a saucepan and dissolve the sugar. Boil, without stirring, until golden. Reduce the heat. Remove from the heat, stand back, and add the cream. Heat gently until the caramel dissolves. Allow to cool.

4 For the Chantilly cream, pour the cream into a bowl, and whip until soft peaks form. Add the icing sugar and vanilla essence, and continue whipping until stiff peaks form. Chill in the refrigerator.

5 Butter a baking tray and heat the grill. Peel and core the pears. Thinly slice, keeping attached at the stalk end. With your fingers, flatten, transfer to the tray, brush with lemon and sprinkle with sugar. Grill until caramelized.

6 Transfer the pastry cases to plates, and place Chantilly cream and a pear fan in each. Pour a little cold caramel sauce over each fan, and partially cover with the pastry lids.

Apricot turnovers

Filo is a multi-purpose pastry and not nearly as hard to work with as you might think. These triangles have a filling of apricots cooked with a mild blend of spices.

• serves 24

• prep 35–40 mins
• cook 30–40 mins

❄

• up to 4 weeks

Ingredients

500g (1lb 2oz) apricots	pinch of ground nutmeg
zest of 1 lemon	pinch of ground cloves
200g (7oz) caster sugar	225g pack of filo pastry
1 tsp ground cinnamon	175g (6oz) unsalted butter

1 For the apricot filling, cut each apricot in half around the stone. Using both hands, give a quick, sharp twist to each half to loosen it from the stone. Scoop out the stone with a knife and discard. Cut each half into 4–5 pieces. Grate the zest from half of the lemon onto a plate.

2 In a saucepan, combine the apricots, lemon zest, three-quarters of the sugar, cinnamon, nutmeg, and cloves. Add 2 tablespoons of water. Cook gently, stirring occasionally, for 20–25 minutes until the mixture thickens to the consistency of jam. Transfer to a bowl and allow to cool.

3 Preheat the oven to 200°C (400°F/Gas 6). Lay a damp, clean tea towel on the work surface, unroll the filo pastry sheets onto the towel, and cut them lengthways in half. Cover them with a second damp, clean towel.

4 Melt the butter in a small pan. Take a half sheet of dough from the pile and set it lengthways on the work surface. Lightly brush the left-hand side of the sheet with butter, and fold the other half over on top. Brush the strip of dough with more butter.

5 Spoon 1–2 teaspoons of the cooled filling onto the strip of dough about 2.5cm (1in) from one end. Do not put too much apricot filling in each turnover, or they will burst during cooking. Fold a corner of the dough strip over the filling to meet the other edge of dough, forming a triangle. Continue folding the strip over and over, to form a triangle with the filling inside. Set the triangle on a baking tray with the final edge underneath, and cover the tray with a damp, clean tea towel. Make sure you have closed the corners tightly so the filling does not leak.

6 Continue making triangles with the remaining filo pastry sheets, filling and arranging them on baking trays, and keeping them covered with damp, clean tea towels. Brush the top of each triangle with butter, and sprinkle with the remaining sugar. Bake for 12–15 minutes until golden brown and flaky. With a palette knife, transfer the turnovers to a wire rack to cool slightly, and serve warm or at room temperature.

Tarta di nata

These bite-sized custard pastries are a Portuguese favourite.

Ingredients

30g (1oz) plain flour,
   plus extra for dusting
500g (1lb 2oz) puff pastry, shop-bought
500ml (16fl oz) milk
1 cinnamon stick

1 large piece lemon zest
4 egg yolks
100g (3½oz) caster sugar
1 tbsp cornflour

1 Preheat the oven to 220°C (425°F/Gas 7). On a floured work surface, roll out the puff pastry to a 40 x 30cm (16 x 12in) rectangle. Roll up the pastry from the long end nearest you to make a log. Trim the ends. Cut the pastry into 16 equal-sized slices.

2 Take a piece of rolled pastry and tuck the loose end underneath it. Lay it down and lightly roll into a thin circle, about 10cm (4in) in diameter, turning it over only once to ensure a natural curve to the finished pastry. You should be left with a shallow bowl type piece of pastry. Use your thumbs to press it into a muffin tin, ensuring it is well-shaped to the tin. Take a fork and lightly prick the bottom. Repeat the process with the rest of the pastries. Leave in the refrigerator, while you make the filling.

3 Heat the milk, cinnamon stick, and lemon zest in a heavy saucepan. When the milk starts to boil, take it off the heat.

4 In a bowl, whisk together the egg yolks, sugar, flour, and cornflour until it forms a thick paste. Remove the cinnamon stick and the lemon zest from the hot milk, and pour the milk gradually over the egg yolk mixture, whisking constantly. Return the custard to the cleaned-out pan and place over medium heat, whisking constantly, until it thickens. When it does, take it immediately off the heat.

5 Fill each pastry case, two-thirds full, with the custard and bake at the top of the oven for 20–25 minutes until the custards are puffed and blackened in places on the surface. Remove from the oven and allow to cool. The custards will deflate slightly, but this is quite normal. Leave for at least 10–15 minutes before eating warm or cold.

Chocolate orange profiteroles

Orange and chocolate have always been a classic combination, but the orange liqueur here brings a lovely depth of flavour.

• serves 6

• prep 20 mins
• cook 35–40 mins

• piping bag and small nozzle (optional)

• up to 12 weeks, unfilled

Ingredients

50g (1¾oz) butter,
   plus extra for greasing
100g (3½oz) plain flour
2 large eggs, lightly beaten

For the chocolate sauce
150g (5½oz) dark chocolate,
   broken into pieces

300ml (10fl oz) single cream
2 tbsp golden syrup
1 tbsp Grand Marnier

For the filling
500ml (16fl oz) double cream
zest of 1 large orange
2 tbsp Grand Marnier

1 Preheat the oven to 220°C (425°F/Gas 7). Lightly grease 2 baking trays. Melt the butter with 300ml (10fl oz) water in a pan, then bring to the boil. As soon as the mixture comes to the boil, remove from the heat, and add the flour. Mix well with a wooden spoon until the mixture is thick and glossy and comes away from the sides of the pan. Gradually beat in the egg, a little at a time until the mixture is smooth, thick, and shiny – it should drop easily off the spoon.

2 Pipe or spoon the mixture into 12 balls, placing them well apart on the baking trays. Bake for 10–15 minutes or until puffed up, then reduce the heat to 190°C (375°F/Gas 5) and bake for a further 20 minutes or until they are crisp and golden. Remove from the oven and make slits in the sides for the steam to escape. Return to the oven for 2–3 minutes so that the centres dry out. Transfer to a wire rack to cool completely.

3 For the chocolate sauce, melt the chocolate, cream, syrup, and Grand Marnier together in a small pan, whisking until the sauce is smooth and glossy. Set aside. For the filling, whisk the cream, orange zest, and Grand Marnier in a bowl until just thicker than soft peaks. Fill the profiteroles with the cream using a piping bag or teaspoon. Serve the profiteroles with the hot sauce spooned over.

Cardamom custard filo tartlets

These crisp, crunchy filo cases are full of just-set delicately spiced custard, and are the perfect way to end a Middle Eastern feast. These little tartlets are best eaten on the day they are made.

• makes 6

• prep 15 mins
• cook 15–20 mins

• 6-hole deep (6cm/2½in) muffin tin

Ingredients

For the filling
225ml (7½fl oz) full-fat milk
150ml (5fl oz) double cream
6 cardamom pods, crushed
plain flour, for dusting
2 eggs
30g (1oz) caster sugar
icing sugar, for dusting

For the pastry
3 sheets ready-made filo pastry
25g (scant 1oz) unsalted butter, melted

1 Preheat the oven to 190°C (375°F/Gas 5). Heat the milk, cream, and cardamom pods in a heavy-based saucepan to boiling point. Turn off the heat and leave the cardamom to infuse.

2 On a well-floured surface, lay out 1 sheet of the filo pastry. Brush the surface of the pastry with a little melted butter, and cover with a second layer. Brush the second layer with more melted butter and cover with a third layer. Cut the pastry into 6 equal pieces.

3 Brush the insides of the muffin tin with a little melted butter. Take a piece of the layered filo and use it to line the muffin mould, pushing it into the sides. The pastry should be ruffled and stick up over the edges in places. Do this with all 6 pieces of pastry. Repeat the layering process with the remaining sheets of pastry until you have 6 filo cases. Brush the pastry edges with any remaining butter and cover the tin with the damp tea towel.

4 For the custard, reheat the milk mixture gently over a medium heat, but do not allow it to boil. Whisk together the eggs and caster sugar in a large bowl. Pour the milk mixture into the whisked eggs and cream through a sieve to remove the cardamom. Whisk the mixture together and transfer it to a jug.

5 Pour the custard into the tart cases and bake for 15–20 minutes until the pastry is crisp at the edges and the custard is just set in the middle. Set the tarts aside to cool in their tins for 10 minutes before removing to cool completely on a wire rack. Dust the tartlets with a little icing sugar before serving.

Apple and almond galettes

Elegant and impressive, these galettes are deceptively simple to make.
The sprinkling of sugar adds a caramelized flavour to the apples.

• makes 8

• prep 25–30 mins,
  plus chilling
• cook 20–30 mins

Ingredients

plain flour, for dusting
600g (1lb 5oz) ready-made puff pastry
215g (7½oz) marzipan
1 lemon

8 small, sharp dessert apples
50g (1¾oz) granulated sugar
icing sugar, for dusting

1 Lightly flour a work surface. Roll out half the pastry to a 35cm (14in) square, about 3mm (⅛in) thick. Using a 15cm (6in) plate as a guide, cut out 4 rounds. Sprinkle 2 baking trays with water. Set the rounds on a tray, and prick each with a fork, avoiding the edge. Repeat with the remaining dough. Chill for 15 minutes. Divide the marzipan into 8 portions, and roll each into a ball.

2 Spread a sheet of baking parchment on the work surface. Set a ball of marzipan on the parchment, and cover with another sheet of parchment. Roll out the marzipan to a 12cm (5in) round between the sheets. Set on top of a pastry round, leaving a border of 1cm (½in). Repeat with the remaining marzipan and pastry rounds. Chill, until ready to bake.

3 Cut the lemon in half and squeeze the juice from one half into a small bowl. Peel, halve, and core the apples; then cut into thin slices. Drop the slices into the lemon juice, and toss.

4 Preheat the oven to 220°C (425°F/Gas 7). Arrange the apple slices, overlapping them slightly, in an attractive spiral over the marzipan rounds. Leave a thin border of pastry dough around the edge. Bake the galettes for 15–20 minutes until the pastry edges have risen around the marzipan and are light golden. Sprinkle the apples evenly with the sugar.

5 Return to the oven and continue baking for 5–10 minutes or until the apples are golden brown, caramelized around the edges, and just tender when tested with the tip of a small knife. Transfer to warmed serving plates, dust with a little icing sugar, and serve immediately.

Pains au chocolat

Golden, flaky rolls, still warm from the oven and oozing with melted chocolate, make the ultimate weekend treat.

• makes 8

• prep 1 hour, plus chilling and rising
• cook 15–20 mins

• up to 4 weeks, unbaked

Ingredients

300g (10oz) strong white bread flour, plus extra for dusting
½ tsp salt
30g (1oz) caster sugar
2½ tsp dried yeast
vegetable oil, for greasing

250g (9oz) unsalted butter, chilled
1 egg, beaten, for glazing

For the filling
200g (7oz) dark chocolate

1 Place the flour, salt, sugar, and yeast in a large bowl, and stir to blend well. Using a table knife, mix in enough warm water, a little at a time, to form a soft dough. Knead on a lightly floured surface until the dough becomes elastic under your hands. Place back in the bowl, cover with lightly oiled cling film, and chill for 1 hour.

2 Roll the dough out into a rectangle that measures 30 x 15cm (12 x 6in). Squash the chilled butter with a rolling pin, keeping the pat shape, until 1cm (½in) thick. Place the butter in the centre of the dough, and fold the dough over it. Chill for 1 hour.

3 Roll out the dough on a lightly floured surface to a 30 x 15cm (12 x 6in) rectangle. Fold the right third to the centre, then the left third over the top. Chill for 1 hour until firm. Repeat the rolling, folding, and chilling twice. Wrap in cling film and chill overnight.

4 Divide the dough into 4 equal pieces and roll each out into a rectangle, about 10 x 40cm (4 x 16in). Cut each piece in half, to give 8 rectangles approximately 10 x 20cm (4 x 8in). Cut the chocolate into 16 even-sized strips. Two 100g bars can be easily divided into 8 strips each. Mark each piece of pastry along the long edge at one-third and two-thirds stages.

5 Put a piece of chocolate at the one-third mark, and fold the short end of the dough over it to the two-thirds mark. Now place a second piece of chocolate on top of the folded edge at the two-thirds mark, brush the dough next to it with beaten egg and fold the other side of the dough into the centre, making a triple-layered parcel with strips of chocolate tucked in on either side. Seal all the edges together to prevent the chocolate from oozing out while cooking.

6 Line a baking tray with parchment, place the pastries on it, cover and leave to rise in a warm place for 1 hour until puffed up and nearly doubled in size. Preheat the oven to 220°C (425°F/Gas 7). Brush the pastries with beaten egg and bake in the oven for 10 minutes, then reduce the oven temperature to 190°C (375°F/Gas 5). Bake for another 5–10 minutes or until golden brown.

Hot cross buns

Delicate and crispy on the outside, these little treats filled with fruit and spices are traditionally eaten at Easter.

Ingredients

200ml (7fl oz) milk
50g (1¾oz) unsalted butter
1 tsp vanilla extract
2 tsp dried yeast
100g (3½oz) caster sugar
500g (1lb 2oz) strong white bread flour, sifted, plus extra for dusting
1 tsp salt
2 tsp mixed spice

1 tsp cinnamon
1 egg, beaten, plus 1 extra for glazing
150g (5½oz) mixed dried fruit (raisins, sultanas, and mixed peel)
vegetable oil, for greasing

For the paste
3 tbsp plain flour
3 tbsp caster sugar

1 Heat the milk, butter, and vanilla extract in a pan until the butter is just melted. Cool until tepid. Whisk in the yeast and 1 tablespoon of sugar. Cover for 10 minutes until it froths.

2 Place the remaining sugar, flour, salt, and spices into a bowl. Mix in the egg. Add the milk mixture and form a dough. Knead for 10 minutes on a floured surface. Press the dough out into a rectangle, scatter over the dried fruit, and knead briefly to combine.

3 Place in an oiled bowl, cover with cling film, and leave in a warm place for 1–2 hours until doubled in size. Turn out onto a floured surface, knock it back, divide into 10–12 pieces, and roll into balls. Line 2 baking trays with parchment and place the buns on them. Cover with cling film and leave to prove for 1–2 hours.

4 Preheat the oven to 220°C (425°F/Gas 7). Brush the buns with the beaten egg. For the paste, mix the flour and sugar with water to make it spreadable. Place it into the piping bag and pipe crosses on the buns. Bake in the top shelf of the oven for 15–20 minutes. Remove to a wire rack and allow to cool for 15 minutes.

Croissants aux amandes

These frangipane-stuffed pastries are light and delicious, and the crispy, flaked almonds lend a wonderful crunch.

• makes 12

• prep 1 hour, plus chilling and rising
• cook 15–20 mins

• up to 4 weeks, unbaked

Ingredients

300g (10oz) strong white bread flour, plus extra for dusting
½ tsp salt
30g (1oz) caster sugar
2½ tsp dried yeast
vegetable oil, for greasing
250g (9oz) unsalted butter, chilled
1 egg, beaten, for the glazing
50g (1¾oz) flaked almonds
icing sugar, to serve

For the almond paste
25g (scant 1oz) unsalted butter, at room temperature
75g (2½oz) caster sugar
75g (2½oz) ground almonds
2–3 tbsp milk, if needed

1 Place the flour, salt, sugar, and yeast in a large bowl, and stir to blend well. Mix in warm water, a little at a time, to form a soft dough. Knead on a lightly floured surface until the dough becomes elastic. Place back in the bowl, cover with lightly oiled cling film, and chill for 1 hour.

2 Roll the dough out into a rectangle that measures 30 x 15cm (12 x 6in). Squash the chilled butter with a rolling pin, keeping the pat shape, until 1cm (½in) thick. Place the butter in the centre of the dough and fold the dough over it. Chill for 1 hour.

3 Roll out the dough on a lightly floured surface to a 30 x 15cm (12 x 6in) rectangle. Fold the right third to the centre, then the left third over the top. Chill for 1 hour until firm. Repeat the rolling, folding, and chilling twice. Wrap in cling film and chill overnight.

4 For the almond paste, cream the butter and sugar together, and blend in the ground almonds. Roll half the dough out on a floured surface to a 12 x 36cm (5 x 14½in) rectangle. Cut into three 12cm (5in) squares, then cut diagonally to make 6 triangles. Repeat with the remaining dough.

5 Spread a spoonful of the paste onto each triangle, leaving a 2cm (¾in) border along the 2 longest sides. Brush the borders with beaten egg. Roll the croissants up carefully from the longest side towards the opposite point. Line 2 baking trays with parchment and place the croissants on them. Cover and leave in a warm place for 1 hour until doubled in size.

6 Preheat the oven to 220°C (425°F/Gas 7). Brush the croissants with beaten egg. Sprinkle with flaked almonds. Bake for 10 minutes, then reduce the temperature to 190°C (375°F/Gas 5). Bake for 5–10 minutes until golden. Cool, and dust with icing sugar to serve.

Brioche buns

Light and tender, these bite-sized buns are traditionally known in France as brioche à tête, for obvious reasons.

• makes 10

• prep 45–50 mins,
  plus rising
  and proving
• cook 15–20 mins

• 10 x 7.5cm (3in)
  brioche moulds

❄

• up to 8 weeks

Ingredients

2½ tsp dried yeast
2 tbsp caster sugar
5 eggs, beaten,
   plus 1 egg, beaten, for glazing
375g (13oz) strong white bread flour,
   plus extra for dusting

1½ tsp salt, plus ½ tsp salt, for glazing
vegetable oil, for greasing
175g (6oz) unsalted butter, diced
   and at room temperature,
   plus extra for greasing

1 Whisk together the yeast, 1 teaspoon sugar, and 2 tablespoons of warm water. Leave for 10 minutes, then add the eggs. In a large bowl, sift together the flour and salt, and add the remaining sugar. Make a well in the flour and pour in the eggs and yeast mixture. Use a fork and then your hands to bring the dough together; it will be quite sticky.

2 Turn out the dough onto a lightly floured work surface. Knead the dough for 10 minutes until elastic but still sticky. Put in an oiled bowl and cover with cling film. Leave to rise in a warm place for 2–3 hours.

3 Gently knock back the dough on a lightly floured work surface. Scatter one-third of the diced butter over the surface of the dough. Fold the dough over the butter and knead gently for 5 minutes. Repeat until all the butter is absorbed and no streaks of butter show.

4 Brush the brioche moulds with melted butter and set them on a baking tray. Divide the dough in half. Roll 1 piece of dough into a cylinder, 5cm (2in) in diameter, and cut it into 5 pieces. Repeat with the remaining dough. Roll each piece of dough into a smooth ball.

5 Pinch one-quarter of each ball, almost dividing it from the remaining dough, to form the head. Holding the head, lower each ball into a mould, twisting and pressing the head onto the base. Cover with a dry, clean tea towel and leave to prove in a warm place for 30 minutes.

6 Preheat the oven to 220°C (425°F/Gas 7). Mix the egg and salt for glazing. Brush the brioches with the glaze. Bake for 15–20 minutes until brown and hollow sounding. Unmould and cool on a wire rack.

Index

A

almonds
  almond crescents 228–9
  almond paste 228–9, 248–9
  apple and almond galettes 242–3
  berry friands 88–9
  biscotti 180–1
  chocolate biscuit cake 184–5
  croissants aux amandes 248–9
  mince pies 190–1
  orange and pistachio cake 60–1
  panforte 160–1
  plum and almond friands 74–5
  raspberry, lemon, and almond bake
    162–3
  raspberry macarons 200–1
  strawberries and cream macarons
    210–11
  tangerine macarons 224–5
apples
  apple and almond galettes 242–3
  apple muffins 62–3
  cinnamon, apple, and sultana cupcakes
    64–5
  toffee apple traybake 164–5
apricots
  apricot crumble shortbread 168–9
  apricot pastries 216–17
  apricot turnovers 234–5

B

baking powder 6
baklava 214–15
ball game mini cakes 126–7
bananas
  banana and chocolate chip muffins
    68–9
  banana and nutella crumble tartlets
    204–5
  mini banana and chocolate topped
    cheesecakes 110–11
berry friands 88–9

biscotti 180–1
  pistachio and orange biscotti 186–7
biscuit-based crusts 194–5
blueberries
  berry friands 88–9
  blueberry and pistachio angel cupcakes
    72–3
  blueberry muffins 86–7
  lemon and blueberry muffins 94–5
Brazil nuts: chocolate truffles 202–3
bridal lace cupcakes 136
brioche buns 250–1
brownies
  double chocolate brownies 144–5
  sour cherry and chocolate brownies
    176–7
  toffee brownies 148–9
brushwork embroidery 49
buns see under mini cakes; patisserie
butter 6
buttercream icing 38
  chocolate 98–9
  coffee 84–5, 172–3
  lemon 64–5, 76–7
  piping 40, 41, 44–5, 100–1
  tangerine 224–5
  vanilla 30, 38, 66–7, 124–5, 134–5
butterflies and blossoms 96–7

C

cake pops 36
  Christmas cake pops 138
  pirate cake pops 140
  princess cake pops 141
  scary cake pops 139
  wedding cake pops 137
cake tins
  cake pop 37
  preparing and lining 26
cakes
  crumb coating 53
cakes, small see cake pops; mini cakes;

mini bakes; slices
cannoli 222–3
caramel sauce 232–3
cardamom tartlets 240–1
Chantilly cream 232–3
cheesecakes: mini banana and chocolate
  topped cheesecakes 110–11
cherries
  cherry and coconut cupcakes 80–1
  cherry flapjacks 156–7
  chocolate truffles 202–3
  Florentine slices 158–9
  sour cherry and chocolate brownies
    176–7
chestnut purée: Mont Blancs 226–7
chocolate
  banana and chocolate chip muffins
    68–9
  buttercream icing 98–9
  cake pops 36
  cannoli 222–3
  cherry flapjacks 156–7
  chocolate and hazelnut brownies
    166–7
  chocolate and toffee shortbread 174–5
  chocolate and vanilla whoopie pies
    124–5
  chocolate biscuit cake 184–5
  chocolate brittle 182–3
  chocolate cupcakes 60–1
  chocolate éclairs 198–9
  chocolate fondants 106–7
  chocolate frosted cupcakes 98–9
  chocolate fudge cake balls 132–3
  chocolate muffins 78–9
  chocolate orange profiteroles 238–9
  chocolate palmiers 206–7
  chocolate truffles 202–3
  Christmas cake pops 138
  double chocolate brownies 144–5
  Florentine slices 158–9
  ganache 48
  icing 132–3

mini banana and chocolate topped
    cheesecakes 110–11
mocha slices 154–5
pains au chocolate 244–5
piping with 43
preparing 27
profiteroles 220–1
sauce 238–9
sour cherry and chocolate brownies
    176–7
triple chocolate crunch bars 170–1
wedding mini cakes 128–9
see also white chocolate
Christmas cake pops 138
churros 218–19
cinnamon
    churros 218–19
    cinnamon, apple and sultana cupcakes
        64–5
    cinnamon palmiers 192–3
    cinnamon rolls 230–1
cocoa: strawberries and cream whoopie
    pies 108–9
coconut
    banana and nutella crumble tartlets
        204–5
    cherry and coconut cupcakes 80–1
    coconut cream tartlets 212–13
    coconut icing 80–1
    Florentine slices 158–9
    raspberry flapjacks 178–9
    white chocolate and coconut snowballs
        134–5
coffee
    buttercream icing 84–5, 172–3
    coffee kisses 172–3
    coffee walnut cupcakes 84–5
    icing 116–17
colourwash 50
coulis, strawberry 122–3
cranberries: chocolate brittle 182–3
cream, whipping 30
cream cheese icing 72–3

cream filling/topping, strawberry 92–3
crème pâtissière 194–5
croissants aux amandes 248–9
crumb coating cakes 53
crumble topping 168–9
cupcakes
    baking 32
    blueberry and pistachio angel cupcakes
        72–3
    bridal lace cupcakes 136
    butterflies and blossoms 96–7
    cherry and coconut cupcakes 80–1
    chocolate cupcakes 60–1
    chocolate frosted cupcakes 98–9
    cinnamon, apple and sultana cupcakes
        64–5
    coffee walnut cupcakes 84–5
    cupcake bouquet 100–1
    filling 35
    lime drizzle cupcakes 70–1
    miniature 33
    orange and lemon cupcakes 76–7
    piping 34
    raspberry cupcakes 90–1
    strawberry and cream cupcakes 92–3
    using cases 32
    vanilla cupcakes 66–7
currants *see* dried fruit
custard pastries 236–7

D

Danish pastries 196–7
    almond crescents 228–9
dates
    sticky date flapjacks 152–3
    sticky toffee puddings 120–1
    sticky walnut buns 116–17
doughnuts, jam 208–9
dried fruit
    cherry flapjacks 156–7
    chocolate biscuit cake 184–5
    chocolate brittle 182–3

cinnamon, apple and sultana cupcakes
    64–5
Florentine slices 158–9
hot cross buns 246–7
mince pies 190–1
rock cakes 114–15
drizzle topping, lime 70–1

E

éclairs, chocolate 198–9
eggs 7
    testing for freshness 28
    whisking egg whites 29
embroidery, brushwork 49

F

figs: panforte 160–1
flapjacks 150–1
    cherry flapjacks 156–7
    raspberry flapjacks 178–9
    sticky date flapjacks 152–3
Florentine slices 158–9
flour 7
fondant, strengthening 52
fondants
    chocolate 106–7
    fondant fancies 118–19
    teddy bear mini cakes 130–1
friands
    berry friands 88–9
    plum and almond friands 74–5

G

ganache 30
glaze topping, lemon 82–3

H

hazelnuts
    chocolate and hazelnut brownies 166–7

chocolate brittle 182–3
mince pies 190–1
panforte 160–1
hot cross buns 246–7

I

icing
    chocolate 132–3
    coconut 80–1
    coffee 84–5, 116–17
    cream cheese 72–3
    lemon 118–19
    royal 39
    sheets 56–7
    vanilla 124–5
see also buttercream icing; fondant

J

jam doughnuts 208–9

L

lemons
    icing 118–19
    lemon and blueberry muffins 94–5
    lemon and poppy seed muffins 82–3
    orange and lemon cupcakes 76–7
    raspberry, lemon, and almond bake
        162–3
lime drizzle cupcakes 70–1

M

macadamia nuts
    chocolate brittle 182–3
    white chocolate and macadamia nut
        blondies 146–7
macarons
    raspberry macarons 200–1
    strawberries and cream macarons
        210–11
    tangerine macarons 224–5
mascarpone: raspberry macarons 200–1
meringues: Mont Blancs 226–7
mince pies 190–1
mini cakes 33

ball game mini cakes 126–7
chocolate fondants 106–7
chocolate fudge cake balls 132–3
fondant fancies 118–19
mini banana and chocolate topped
    cheesecakes 110–11
rock cakes 114–15
sticky toffee puddings 116–17
sticky walnut buns 116–17
strawberry shortcakes 122–3
teddy bear mini cakes 130–1
wedding mini cakes 128–9
Welsh cakes 112–13
white chocolate cakes 104–5
see also whoopie pies
mini bakes
    biscotti 180–1
    chocolate and hazelnut brownies 166–7
    chocolate biscuit cake 184–5
    chocolate brittle 182–3
    coffee kisses 172–3
    double chocolate brownies 144–5
    pistachio and orange biscotti 186–7
    sour cherry and chocolate brownies
        176–7
    toffee brownies 148–9
    white chocolate and macadamia nut
        blondies 146–7
mixed peel
    cannoli 222–3
    Florentine slices 158–9
    hot cross buns 246–7
    mince pies 190–1
    panforte 160–1
mocha slices 154–5
Mont Blancs 226–7
muffins
    apple muffins 62–3
    banana and chocolate chip muffins 68–9
    blueberry muffins 86–7
    chocolate muffins 78–9
    lemon and blueberry muffins 94–5
    lemon and poppy seed muffins 82–3

N O

nutella: banana and nutella crumble
    tartlets 204–5

oranges
    orange and lemon cupcakes 76–7
    pistachio and orange biscotti 186–7

P

pains au chocolate 244–5
palmiers
    chocolate palmiers 206–7
    cinnamon 192–3
panforte 160–1
pastry
    for cannoli 222–3
    choux 220–1, 238–9
    flaky 244–5
    puff 216–17
    sweet shortcrust 204–5, 212–13
patisserie
    almond crescents 228–9
    apricot pastries 216–17
    apricot turnovers 234–5
    baklava 214–15
    brioche buns 250–1
    cannoli 222–3
    chocolate orange profiteroles 238–9
    chocolate palmiers 206–7
    chocolate truffles 202–3
    churros 218–19
    cinnamon palmiers 192–3
    cinnamon rolls 230–1
    croissants aux amandes 248–9
    Danish pastries 196–7
    hot cross buns 246–7
    jam doughnuts 208–9
    Mont Blancs 226–7
    pains au chocolate 244–5
    profiteroles 220–1
    raspberry macarons 200–1
    strawberries and cream macarons
        210–11
    tangerine macarons 224–5
    tarta di nata 236–7
pears: flaky pear tartlets 232–3
pecan nuts
    apple muffins 62–3
    chocolate brittle 182–3
    toffee brownies 148–9
petit fours: mini banana and chocolate

topped cheesecakes 110–11
piping 40-47
    bag and nozzle 31
    buttercream icing 40–1, 44–5
    chocolate 43
    dots and beads 42–3
    filigree 46, 55
    royal icing 42, 46–7
pirate cake pops 140
pistachio nuts
    baklava 214–15
    blueberry and pistachio angel cupcakes
        72–3
    pistachio and orange biscotti 186–7
plum and almond friands 74–5
poppy seeds: lemon and poppy seed
    muffins 82–3
princess cake pops 141
profiteroles 220–1
    chocolate orange profiteroles 238–9

R

raisins see dried fruit
raspberries
    berry friands 88–9
    raspberry, lemon, and almond bake
        162–3
    raspberry cupcakes 90–1
    raspberry flapjacks 178–9
    raspberry macarons 200–1
    raspberry tartlets with crème pâtissière
        194–5
ricotta cheese: cannoli 222–3
rock cakes 114–15
royal icing 39
    piping 42, 46–7, 55

S

sauces
    caramel 232–3
    chocolate 238–9
    toffee 116–17, 164–5
scary cake pops 139
shortbread
    apricot crumble shortbread 168–9
    chocolate and toffee shortbread 174–5

shortcake, strawberry 122–3
slices
    apricot crumble shortbread 168–9
    cherry flapjacks 156–7
    chocolate and toffee shortbread 174–5
    flapjacks 150–1
    Florentine slices 158–9
    mocha slices 154–5
    panforte 160–1
    raspberry, lemon, and almond bake
        162–3
    raspberry flapjacks 178–9
    sticky date flapjacks 152–3
    toffee apple traybake 164–5
    triple chocolate crunch bars 170–1
spices: panforte 160–1
sponging 54
stencilling 47, 126
sticky date flapjacks 152–3
sticky toffee puddings 120–1
sticky walnut buns 116–17
stippling 54
strawberries
    cream filling/topping 92–3
    strawberries and cream macarons
        210–11
    strawberries and cream whoopie pies
        108–9
    strawberry and cream cupcakes 92–3
    strawberry shortcakes 122–3
sugar 6
sugar gems 51
sultanas see dried fruit

T

tangerine macarons 224–5
tarta di nata 236–7
tarts
    apple and almond galettes 242–3
    banana and nutella crumble tartlets
        204–5
    cardamom tartlets 240–1
    coconut cream tartlets 212–13
    flaky pear tartlets 232–3
    mince pies 190–1
    raspberry tartlets with crème pâtissière
        194–5

tarta di nata 236–7
teddy bear mini cakes 130–1
toffee
    chocolate and toffee shortbread 174–5
    sauce 116–17, 164–5
    sticky toffee puddings 120–1
    toffee apple traybake 164–5
    toffee brownies 148–9
traybakes see slices
truffles, chocolate 202–3

V

vanilla
    buttercream icing 30, 38, 134–5
    chocolate and vanilla whoopie pies
        124–5
    vanilla cupcakes 66–7

W

walnuts
    baklava 214–15
    coffee walnut cupcakes 84–5
    sticky walnut buns 116–17
    white chocolate cakes 104–5
wedding cake pops 137
wedding mini cakes 128–9
Welsh cakes 112–13
white chocolate
    cake pops 36
    cherry flapjacks 156–7
    chocolate and toffee shortbread
        174–5
    chocolate brittle 182–3
    double chocolate brownies 144–5
    mini banana and chocolate topped
        cheesecakes 110–11
    raspberry cupcakes 90–1
    triple chocolate crunch bars 170–1
    white chocolate and coconut snowballs
        134–5
    white chocolate and macadamia nut
        blondies 146–7
    white chocolate cakes 104–5
whoopie pies
    chocolate and vanilla 124–5
    strawberries and cream 108–9

Acknowledgments

Dorling Kindersley would like to thank:

The recipe writers and cake decorators: Yvonne Allison, Ah Har Ashley, Anna Guest, Asma Hassan, Mrs J Hough, Carolyn Humphries, Tracy McCue, Sandra Monger, Juliet Monteforte, Amelia Nutting, Catherine Parker, Jean Piercy, Emma Shibli, Karen Sullivan, Penelope Tilston, and Galina Varese.

Photographers: Steve Baxter, Clive Bozzard-Hill, Martin Brigdale, Tony Cambio, Nigel Gibson, Francesco Guillamet, Michael Hart, Adrian Heapy, Jeff Kauck, David Munns, David Murray, Ian O'Leary, Roddy Paine, William Reavell, Gavin Sawyer, William Shaw, Howard Shooter, Carole Tuff, Kieran Watson, Stuart West, and Jon Whitaker.

Michele Clarke for the index.

Lakeland for the donation of equipment.